CHROMEBOOK FOR SENIORS

A Senior's and Beginner's user friendly guide to surfing the web with Google chrome.

William Murphy White

OVERVIEW

A laptop known as a Chromebook is one that is powered by Chrome OS, a thin operating system built around the Google Chrome web browser. Chromebooks are made to be quick, safe, and simple to use. They are frequently a suitable option for elderly, students, and those who use their computers only for web browsing, email, and light productivity tasks because they are usually less expensive than laptops running Windows or macOS.

The following are some of Chromebooks' salient characteristics:

Quick and light: Chromebooks operate smoothly and rapidly even on low-end hardware.

Secure: Chromebooks automatically update themselves to guard against the most recent threats, and Chrome OS was created with security in mind.

Easy to use: Even for those without prior computer experience, Chromebooks are incredibly simple to use.

Cloud-based: The majority of the data on Chromebooks is stored in the cloud, allowing you to access your files from any location and eliminating the risk of data loss in the event that your Chromebook is stolen or lost.

Affordable: Generally speaking, Chromebooks are less costly than laptops running Windows or macOS.

The following are some of the uses for a Chromebook:

Web browsing: Chromebooks are built with the Chrome web browser pre-installed, making them ideal for online browsing.

Check email: Gmail is pre-installed on Chromebooks, making it simple to check your inbox.

Remain connected: Google Chat and Hangouts are pre-installed on Chromebooks, allowing you to video chat and communicate with friends and family.

Work with documents, spreadsheets, and presentations: Google Docs, Sheets, and Slides are built into Chromebooks out of the box, making it simple to create and modify documents, spreadsheets, and presentations.

Store and share data: Google Drive storage is available for 15GB free of charge with Chromebooks, making it simple to store and share files with others.

All things considered, Chromebooks are a fantastic choice for those seeking a cost-effective, quick, safe, and user-friendly laptop.

WHY IS CHROMEBOOK GOOD FOR SENIORS

Seniors might consider Chromebooks for several reasons.

Comfort of Use: Chromebooks are made to be extremely user-friendly, even for people with little prior computer experience. They include all of the necessary programs pre-installed, including Chrome, Gmail, and Google Docs, and offer an easy-to-use UI. Because of this, they are perfect for seniors who are new to computers or who feel uneasy using more complicated operating systems like Windows or macOS.

Safety: Because of the sandboxing feature of Chrome OS, Chromebooks are extremely safe computers. This keeps malware from propagating to other areas of the system since every web page and application operates in a separate, isolated environment. To further ensure that your device is always safe from the most recent attacks,

Chromebooks automatically upgrade to the most recent security patches.

Accessible: Generally speaking, Chromebooks are far less expensive than laptops running Windows or macOS. This is because they don't need as powerful hardware because they are made to be lightweight and efficient. They are therefore an excellent choice for seniors on a tight budget.

Storage via the Cloud: The majority of your data is stored on Chromebooks in the cloud, allowing you to access it on any device and from any location. Seniors who may travel frequently or who want to be able to access their data from a smartphone or tablet will find this to be really helpful.

Adaptability: Web browsing, email, social media, streaming video, and even simple productivity tasks like making documents and spreadsheets may all be done on Chromebooks. Because of this, they're an excellent all-around gadget for seniors who utilize computers for a range of tasks.

Apart from these broad advantages, Chromebooks provide some particular characteristics that make them an excellent choice for elderly people:

Large screens and keyboards: A lot of Chromebooks come with large screens and keyboards, which can help seniors with vision or dexterity problems use them more easily.

Long battery life: Seniors can use Chromebooks for hours without worrying about plugging them in because they usually have a long battery life.

Built-in accessibility features: Seniors with disabilities may find Chromebooks even easier to use thanks to their many built-in accessibility capabilities, which include text-to-speech and screen magnification.

For seniors searching for a cost-effective, safe, and user-friendly laptop, Chromebooks are often a wonderful option. They are an excellent method for seniors to remain in touch with friends and family, learn new things, and take advantage of everything the internet has to offer. They are well-suited for seniors' needs due to their many features.

Setting up your Chromebook book

Your Chromebook setup is a quick and easy process that just takes a few minutes to finish. Here's a how-to manual to get you going:

Step 1: Take out your Chromebook

Unpack your Chromebook carefully and take it out of its package. In the unlikely event that you must return the device for any reason, be sure to save all the package materials.

Step 2: Plug in the power source

Find the power supply that was included with your Chromebook. The Chromebook's power port, which is often located on the side or close to the rear of the device, is compatible with the little connector on one end of the adapter. The adaptor will have a regular AC plug on the other end that plugs into a wall socket. Attach the power adapter to the wall outlet and the Chromebook.

Step 3: Switch the Chromebook on

On your Chromebook, locate the power button (typically on the right side or close to the top edge) and press and hold it.

When the Chromebook boots up, the Google logo will appear.

Step 4: Adhere to the instructions displayed on the screen.

To finish the setup, adhere to the directions displayed on the screen. This will entail picking your preferred language, adjusting the keyboard, and establishing a Wi-Fi connection.

Step 5: Use your Google Account to Log in

To log into your Chromebook, enter your password and email address associated with your Google Account. You can make a free Google Account if you don't already have one.

Selecting your profile photo is the sixth step.

You will be able to select a profile photo to use on your Chromebook. You have the option to upload your own photo or choose from among the suggested ones.

Step 7: Tailor your Chromebook to your needs

As soon as you log in, you can begin personalizing your Chromebook. This involves configuring your keyboard's settings, language, background, and other options.

Step 8: Install Chrome Web Store apps

You may install a huge selection of apps on your Chromebook from the Chrome Web Store. Just type the app's name into the search field to locate it.

Additionally, you can peruse the apps' many categories, which include productivity, entertainment, and education.

Step 9: Get your Chromebook going!

You can use your Chromebook for a variety of tasks, including working on papers, checking email, and online browsing, once it has been configured. Discover all of the features and apps that your Chromebook has to offer.

* You can get help setting up your Chromebook by going to the Google Chromebook Help Center. YouTube also has videos and tutorials that can be of use. Additionally, the majority of Chromebook makers provide their own support resources.

The Basics of Using a Chromebook

Using the Chrome OS desktop

* The Chrome OS desktop is the main screen of your Chromebook. It is where you

will find all of your apps and files.

* To open an app, simply click on its icon. The app will open in a new window.

* To close an app, click on the X button in the top right corner of the window.

* You can also minimize an app by clicking on the - button in the top right corner of the window. This will hide the app, but it will still be running in the background.

* To maximize an app, click on the □ button in the top right corner of the window. This will

make the app fill the entire screen.

* To move an app window, click and hold on the title bar of the window and drag it to the desired location.

* To resize an app window, click and hold on the bottom right corner of the window and drag it to the desired size.

You can also use the keyboard shortcuts to manage your app windows:

Action | Shortcut

To Open an app: Alt + [number], where [number] is the number of the app in the dock.

To Close an app: Alt + F4. |

To Minimize an app: Alt + -

To Maximise an app: Alt + Enter.

To Move an app window: Alt + Spacebar, and then use the arrow keys to move the window.

To Resize an app window: Alt + Spacebar, and then use the arrow keys to resize the window.

Managing windows

Using a Chromebook to manage Windows is simple and comparable to using Windows on other operating systems. Here are a few simple tasks you can complete on your Chromebook using Windows:

1. Windows Opened and Closed: Opening: Click on an app's icon in the launcher or within the app

to open it. A new window containing the program will open.

Finally: Click the "X" button located in the upper right corner of a window to close it. The window will vanish and the app will close.

2. Windows switching: Alt + Tab: Press the Alt + Tab keyboard combination to navigate between open windows. The following window will open in the sequence that they were opened with each Tab key push.

Housing Icons Clicking: Additionally, you can navigate between windows by clicking on the icons in the taskbar located at the bottom of the screen.

3. Windows Minimization and Maximization: Minimization: Click the "-" button in the upper right corner of a window to make it smaller. The window will resize to fit on the taskbar as a little icon.

Employing: Click the □ button located in the upper right corner of a window to make it fully visible. The window will grow until it completely fills the screen.

4. Windows Resizing: Drag and Drop: To resize the window, click and hold its lower right corner and drag it to the desired location. The window will adjust in size.

5. Snapping Windows: Maximize to Half Screen: Drag a window to its left or right border to make it fill half of the screen in an instant.

Maximize to Full Screen: To make a window fill the screen, drag it to the upper border.

6. Shifting Windows: Drag and Click: To move the window's title bar to a desired spot on the screen, click and hold it. The window will reposition itself.

7. Restoring Reduced Windows: Press the Reduced Icon: To return the window to its original size and location, click on its minimized icon in the taskbar.

You may use many programs and tasks on your Chromebook

more effectively and efficiently by using these simple window management techniques.

Working with the Chrome OS keyboard shortcuts

Chrome OS offers a variety of keyboard shortcuts that can help you navigate your Chromebook more efficiently. Here are some of the most useful shortcuts:

General Shortcuts

Ctrl + Shift + T: Reopen the last closed tab in Chrome.

Ctrl + W: Close the current tab in Chrome.

Alt + Tab: Switch between open windows.

Ctrl + Alt + Esc: Open the Task Manager to view and manage running apps.

Ctrl + F: Find text within the current window.

Ctrl + P: Print the current web page or document.

Ctrl + +: Zoom in on the current web page or document.

Ctrl + -: Zoom out of the current web page or document.

Window Management Shortcuts

Alt + Spacebar: Grab and move the current window.

Alt + Enter: Maximize the current window to full screen.

Alt + -: Minimize the current window to the taskbar.

Alt + [Number]: Switch to the app window corresponding to the number (1-9) in the launcher.

Navigation Shortcuts

Home: Go to the top of the current web page or document.

End: Go to the bottom of the current web page or document.

Up arrow: Scroll one line up in the current web page or document.

Down arrow:Scroll one line down in the current web page or document.

Page Up: Scroll one page up in the current web page or document.

Page Down: Scroll one page down in the current web page or document.

Editing Shortcuts

Ctrl + C: Copy selected text.
Ctrl + X: Cut selected text.

Ctrl + V: Paste copied or cut text.
Ctrl + Z: Undo the last action.
Ctrl + Y: Redo the last undone action.

These are just a few of the many keyboard shortcuts available in Chrome OS. For a complete list of shortcuts, you can visit the Chrome OS Help Center.

Using the Chromebook touchpad

The Chromebook touchpad is a versatile input device that allows you to control your Chromebook with your fingertips. It is similar to a traditional laptop touchpad, but it also supports some unique gestures that can make your Chromebook experience even more efficient.

Basic touchpad gestures

Single tap: Click on an item or open an app.

Double tap: Zoom in on a web page or document.

Two-finger tap: Open the context menu (right-click menu) for an item.

Three-finger tap: Minimize the current window.

Four-finger tap: Switch between open windows.

One-finger drag:Scroll up or down on a web page or document.

Two-finger drag: Zoom in or out on a web page or document.

Three-finger drag: Move the current window.

Four-finger drag: Switch to the next or previous virtual workspace.

Additional touchpad gestures

Two-finger swipe up: Go to the next tab in Chrome.

Two-finger swipe down: Go to the previous tab in Chrome.

Three-finger swipe up: Show all open windows.

Three-finger swipe down: Minimize all open windows.

Three-finger swipe left: Switch to the previous virtual workspace.

Three-finger swipe right: Switch to the next virtual workspace.

Tips for using the Chromebook touchpad

Rest your fingers comfortably on the touchpad.

Use light, smooth strokes for scrolling and dragging.

Click using the touchpad's left or right click button.

You can adjust the touchpad sensitivity in the Settings app.

With a little practice, you'll be using the Chromebook touchpad like a pro in no time.

Using the Chromebook touchscreen

Basic touchscreen gestures

Tap: Click on an item or open an app.

Double tap: Zoom in on a web page or document.

Swipe up or down: Scroll up or down on a web page or document.

Pinch or spread: Zoom in or out on a web page or document.

Slide left or right: Switch between open windows.

Drag and drop: Move items around on the screen.

Additional touchscreen gestures

Two-finger tap: Open the context menu (right-click menu) for an item.

Three-finger tap: Minimize the current window.

Four-finger tap: Show all open windows.
Four-finger swipe up: Go to the next tab in Chrome.

Four-finger swipe down:Go to the previous tab in Chrome.

Four-finger swipe left: Switch to the previous virtual workspace.

Four-finger swipe right: Switch to the next virtual workspace.

Tips for using the Chromebook touchscreen

Use light, gentle taps and swipes.

Pinch or spread with two fingers, not one.

Use your fingers to drag and drop items around the screen.

You can adjust the touchscreen sensitivity in the Settings app.

With a little practice, you'll be using the Chromebook touchscreen like a pro in no time.

Customizing your Chromebook

You may improve and personalize your Chromebook's experience by customizing it. Here are a few methods for personalizing your Chromebook:

1. To alter the wallpaper on your Chromebook, right-click anywhere on the desktop and

choose "Set wallpaper" from the menu. You can upload your own pictures or select from a selection of pre-made ones.

2. Modify your theme: Your Chromebook's general color scheme, which includes the window borders, toolbars, and menus, can be altered. To select from a number of pre-made themes or to design your own unique colors, go to Settings > Personalization > Set wallpaper & style > Color and theme.

3. **Modify the cursor:** Your cursor's appearance, including

its size, color, and animation style, can be altered. To change these settings, navigate to Settings > Accessibility > Cursor and touchpad.

4. Set up your applications: To make it simpler to locate the apps you use most frequently, you can rearrange the icons in the launcher, which is the dock-like area at the bottom of the screen. An app icon can be moved by clicking and holding it.

5. *Install and uninstall apps:** Adding or removing apps from

your Chromebook is a simple process. Navigate to the Chrome Web Store and search for the desired app to add. Apps can be removed by performing a right-click on their launcher icon and choosing "Remove from launcher" or "Uninstall."

6. Modify the keyboard's settings: You can adjust the keyboard's settings to your liking by turning on input languages, keyboard shortcuts, and auto-correction. To change these options, navigate to Settings > Advanced > Languages and Inputs.

7. Modify your alert preferences: Notifications from apps and how they appear are both customizable. To change these preferences, navigate to Settings > Privacy and security > Notifications.

8. Modify your display preferences: To fit your demands, you can change the display's brightness, resolution, and scaling on your Chromebook. To change these preferences, navigate to Settings > Advanced > Display.

9. Modify the power management configurations: To increase the lifespan of your Chromebook's battery, you can manage how it consumes power. To change these options, navigate to options > Device > Power.

10. Modify your region and language settings: Your Chromebook's language and region settings are customizable to fit your tastes. To change these options, navigate to Settings > Advanced > Languages and Inputs.

These pointers can help you customize your Chromebook to make it uniquely yours and improve your experience in general.

BROWSING THE WEB WITH CHROME

The following instructions will show you how to launch and close Chrome windows on a Chromebook:

Finding a window in Chrome

A Chrome window can be opened in one of two ways:

1. In the launcher, Click the Chrome icon. The row of icons at the bottom of the screen is this one. Typically, a blue circle

with a white "C" inside is the Chrome icon.

2. On your keyboard, Press Ctrl + N. Even if Chrome is not already active, using this keyboard shortcut will launch a new Chrome window.

Shutting down a Chrome tab

A Chrome window can be closed in one of two ways:

1. In the upper right corner of the window, Click the X button.

2. On your keyboard, Ctrl + W. The active Chrome window can be closed with this keyboard shortcut.

Shutting down every Chrome window

Use the keyboard shortcut **Shift + Ctrl + W** to quickly shut every Chrome window.

Reopening a Chrome window that was closed"

You can use the keyboard shortcut **Ctrl + Shift + T** to reopen a Chrome window that you may have inadvertently closed. The previous closed Chrome window will reopen when you use this keyboard shortcut.

Navigating the web

Navigating the web on a Chromebook is a straightforward process that involves using the Chrome browser and its various features. Here's a guide to help you get around the web efficiently:

Using the address bar

The address bar is the main way to navigate to specific websites on the web. It's located at the top of the Chrome window, typically with a magnifying glass icon on the left. To visit a website, simply type its address into the address bar and press Enter.

Using bookmarks

Bookmarks are shortcuts to websites that you frequently visit. To save a bookmark, click on the star icon in the address bar next to the website you want to bookmark. You can then access your bookmarks by clicking on the three dots icon in the top right corner of the Chrome window and selecting "Bookmarks."

Using search engines

Search engines like Google can help you find websites and information on the web. To use a search engine, simply type your search query into the address bar and press Enter. Chrome will then display a list of websites and other information related to your search query.

Scrolling through pages

To scroll up or down on a web page, use the scroll bar on the right side of the Chrome window. You can also use the scroll wheel on your Chromebook's touchpad or mouse.

Using tabs

Tabs allow you to open multiple websites simultaneously within the same Chrome window. To open a new tab, click on the plus sign (+) next to the currently active tab. To switch between tabs, click on the tab you want to view.

Using extensions

Extensions are small programs that can add new features and functionality to Chrome. You can find extensions in the Chrome Web Store. To install an extension, click on the "Add to Chrome" button next to the extension you want to install.

Using incognito mode

Incognito mode is a privacy mode that prevents Chrome from saving your browsing history, cookies, and site data. To open an incognito window, press Ctrl + Shift + N on your keyboard.

Using the back and forward buttons

The back and forward buttons allow you to navigate back and forth through your browsing history. The back button is the arrow pointing to the left, and the forward button is the arrow pointing to the right. You can also use the keyboard shortcuts Ctrl + Left Arrow to go back and Ctrl + Right Arrow to go forward.

These basic navigation techniques will help you explore and navigate the vast expanse of the World Wide Web with ease on your Chromebook.

Using tabs

Tabs are a feature of web browsers that allow users to open multiple web pages within a single browser window. This can be helpful for multitasking, as it allows users to keep multiple websites open without having to clutter their desktop with multiple windows.

Here are some of the benefits of using tabs:

Increased productivity: Tabs can help users increase their productivity by allowing them to keep multiple websites open at once. This can be helpful for tasks such as research, where users may need to refer to multiple sources at once.

Improved organization: Tabs can help users organize their browsing activity by allowing them to group related websites together. This can make it easier to find the information they need, and it can also help to reduce clutter on their desktop.

Reduced distractions: Tabs can help to reduce distractions by keeping multiple websites in a single window. This can help users to focus on the task at hand, and it can also help to prevent them from getting sucked into unrelated websites.

Here are some of the ways you can use tabs:

* **Open a new tab:** You can open a new tab by clicking on the plus (+) sign in the tab bar. You can also open a new tab by pressing Ctrl+T on your keyboard.

* **Switch between tabs:** You can switch between tabs by clicking on the tab you want to view. You can also switch between tabs by pressing Ctrl+Tab or Ctrl+Shift+Tab on your keyboard.

* **Close a tab:** You can close a tab by clicking on the X button in the tab bar. You can also close a tab by pressing Ctrl+W on your keyboard.

* **Reload a tab:** You can reload a tab by clicking on the reload button in the address bar. You can also reload a tab by pressing F5 on your keyboard.

* **Pin a tab:** You can pin a tab to keep it open at all times, even if you close all other tabs. To pin a tab, right-click on it and select Pin tab.

* **Unpin a tab**: To unpin a tab, right-click on it and select. Unpin tab.

Bookmarking websites

Here are some tips for bookmarking websites on a Chromebook:

Bookmark websites that you use frequently: This will make it easier to find them later.

Organize your bookmarks by category: This will make it

easier to find the bookmarks you need.

Use descriptive bookmark names: This will make it easier to remember what the bookmark is for.

Delete bookmarks that you no longer use: This will help to keep your bookmark list clutter-free.

Here are some additional tips for managing your bookmarks on a Chromebook:

* You can use the search bar in the Bookmark Manager to find specific bookmarks.

* You can create folders to organize your bookmarks.

* You can right-click on a bookmark and select "Open in new tab" to open the bookmark in a new tab.

* You can right-click on a bookmark and select "Delete bookmark" to delete the bookmark.

Searching the web

Here are some tips for searching the web on a Chromebook:

Use a descriptive query: The more specific your query is, the better the search results will be.

Use quotation marks to search for exact phrases: If you want to search for an exact phrase, put it in quotation marks.

Use Boolean operators to refine your search: You can

use Boolean operators, such as AND, OR, and NOT, to refine your search results. For example, if you want to search for websites that contain the words "Chromebook" and "reviews," you would enter "Chromebook AND reviews" into the search bar.

Use Google Search operators: Google Search supports a number of operators that can help you refine your search results. For example, you can use the site: operator to search for websites on a specific domain, or the intitle: operator to search for websites that have a specific phrase in their title.

Use advanced search options: Google Search also has a number of advanced search options that you can use to refine your results. To access these options, click on the "Tools" menu and select "Advanced search."

Here are some additional tips for searching the web on a Chromebook:

* **Use the Chrome Web Store** to install extensions that

can help you with your search. For example, there are extensions that can help you block ads, or that can show you related search results.

* **Use Chrome's built-in search features.** For example, you can search for a specific word or phrase on a web page by pressing Ctrl + F and entering the word or phrase into the search bar.

* **Use a different search engine.** If you are not satisfied with the results from Google Search, you can try using a

different search engine, such as DuckDuckGo or Bing.

MANAGING EMAIL WITH GMAIL

Signing up for a Gmail Account

Here are the steps on how to sign up for a Gmail account:

1. Go to the Gmail sign-in page: https://accounts.google.com/

2. Click on the "Create account" button.

3. Enter your first and last name.

4. Choose a username for your Gmail account. This will be the part of your email address that comes before the "@gmail.com" part.

5. Create a password for your Gmail account. Your password must be at least eight characters long and contain a mix of upper and lowercase letters, numbers, and symbols.

6. Confirm your password by entering it again.

7. Enter your birthday and gender. This information is optional, but it will help Google to personalize your experience.

8. Enter your phone number. This is optional, but it will help Google to verify your account and keep it secure.

9. Choose your country of residence.

10. Click on the "I agree to the Google Terms of Service and Privacy Policy" checkbox.

11. Click on the "Next" button.

12. You will now be prompted to verify your phone number. If you entered your phone number in step 6, you will receive a text message from Google with a verification code. Enter the verification code into the field provided and click on the "Verify" button.

13. Once you have verified your phone number, you will be able to sign in to your new Gmail account.

Here are some additional tips for signing up for a Gmail account:

* Use a strong password that you will not forget.

* Do not share your password with anyone.

* Use a different email address for non-personal accounts.

* Be careful about what information you share online

Sending And Receiving Emails

Sure, here are the steps on how to send and receive emails in Gmail:

To send an email:

1. Click on the "Compose" button in the top left corner of the Gmail window.

2. In the "To" field, enter the email address of the person you want to send the email to. You can also add multiple recipients by separating their email addresses with commas.

3. In the "Subject" field, enter a brief summary of what the email is about.

4. In the body of the email, type your message.

5. Click on the "Send" button.

To receive an email:

1. Gmail will automatically check for new emails every few minutes. You can also check for new emails manually by clicking

on the "Refresh" button in the top left corner of the Gmail window.

2. New emails will appear in your inbox. Click on an email to open it.

3. To reply to an email, click on the "Reply" button.

4. To forward an email, click on the "Forward" button.

Here are some additional tips for sending and receiving emails in Gmail:

* Use a clear and concise subject line.

* Proofread your email before you send it.

* Use a professional tone and avoid using slang or abbreviations.

* Attach files to your emails if necessary.

Organizing your inbox

Organizing your Gmail inbox can help you manage your email more effectively and make it easier to find the messages you need. Here are some tips for organizing your inbox:

Use labels to categorize your emails. Labels are like folders, but they can be more flexible. You can apply multiple labels to an email, and you can search for emails by label. To create a new label, click on the "More" button in the left sidebar and select "Create new label." Then, enter a name for the label and click on the "Create" button.

To apply a label to an email, select the email and then click on the "Labels" button in the toolbar. Then, select the label you want to apply from the list.

Use filters to automatically organize your emails. Filters are rules that you can create to automatically move emails to specific labels or folders. For example, you could create a filter to move all emails from your boss to a "Boss" label, or to move all emails with the subject "Important" to a "To-Do" folder. To create a new filter, click on the "Settings" gear in the top right corner of the Gmail window and select "See all settings." Then, scroll down to the "Filters" section and click on the "Create a new filter" link. Enter the criteria for your filter and then click on the "Create filter" button.

Use stars to mark important emails. Stars are a quick way to mark important emails so that you can find them easily later. To start an email, simply click on the star icon next to the email in your inbox. To see all of your starred emails, click on the "Starred" label in the left sidebar.

Use search to find specific emails. Gmail's search feature is very powerful and can help you find emails quickly and easily. To search for emails, enter your search query into the search bar at the top of the Gmail window. Gmail will then display a list of emails that match your query.

Use snooze to postpone emails. If you don't have time to deal with an email right away, you can snooze it to have it come back to your inbox later. To snooze an email, select the email and then click on the "Snooze" button in the toolbar. You can choose to snooze the email for later today, tomorrow, this week, or next week.

Use multiple inboxes. If you receive a lot of email, you may want to consider using multiple inboxes to help you manage it. For example, you could create a separate inbox for work emails, personal emails, and social media notifications. To create a new inbox, click on the "More" button in the left sidebar and select "Create new inbox." Then, enter a name for the inbox and click on the "Create" button.

By following these tips, you can organise your Gmail inbox and make it easier to manage your email.

STAYING CONNECTED WITH GOOGLE CHAT AND HANGOUTS

Setting up a Google Chat Account

Since Google Chat is an integrated feature within your Google Account, you don't need to create a separate account specifically for Chat. You can access it directly using your existing Google Account credentials.

To sign in to Google Chat on your computer, you can follow these steps:

1. Open a web browser and go to https://accounts.google.com/

2. Sign in to your Google Account using your email address and password.

3. Once you're signed in, you'll see the Gmail interface. Click on the Chat icon located in the top left corner of the screen, next to the Google logo.

4. The Chat window will open, and you'll be able to start chatting with your contacts.

If you're using a mobile device, you can download the Google Chat app from the App Store or Google Play Store. Once you've installed the app, sign in using your Google Account credentials. You'll then be able to access your Chat conversations from your mobile device.

Chatting with friends and family

Chatting with friends and family can be a great way to stay connected, share experiences, and just have fun. Here are some tips for chatting with friends and family online:

Choose the right platform: There are many different platforms for chatting online, so it's important to choose one that you and your friends and family are all comfortable with. Some popular options include Facebook Messenger, WhatsApp, and Google Chat.

Be mindful of your audience: When chatting with friends and family, it's important to be mindful of your audience. Avoid sharing anything that you wouldn't want everyone to see.

Keep it light and fun: Chatting should be a fun and enjoyable experience. Keep your conversations light and upbeat, and avoid getting into any serious or controversial topics.

Be patient: It can sometimes take time to get the hang of online chatting. Be patient with yourself and with your friends and family.

Use emojis and GIFs: Emojis and GIFs can be a great way to add personality to your conversations and make them more fun.

Schedule regular chat times: It can be helpful to schedule regular chat times with your friends and family. This will help you stay connected and make sure that you have time to catch up.

Share photos and videos: Sharing photos and videos is a great way to share your life with your friends and family.

Play online games: Playing online games together can be a fun way to bond with your friends and family.

Join online communities: There are many online communities that revolve around specific interests. Joining a community can be a great way to connect with people who share your interests.

Chatting with friends and family online can be a great way to stay connected and have fun. By following these tips, you can make sure that your online chats are enjoyable and rewarding.

Making video calls with Hangouts

Here are the steps on how to make video calls with Hangouts:

1. Open the Hangouts app or go to hangouts.google.com.

2. If you're not signed in to Hangouts, sign in using your Google Account credentials.

3. Click on the "Start a video call" button.

4. Enter the email address or phone number of the person you want to call.

5. Click on the "Video call" button.

6. Once the person you're calling answers, you'll see their video feed on the left side of the

screen, and your own video feed on the right side of the screen.

7. To end the video call, click on the "End call" button.

Here are some additional tips for making video calls with Hangouts:

* Make sure that your computer has a webcam and microphone.

* Make sure that you have a good internet connection.

* Find a quiet place to make your call.

* Use headphones or a headset to improve audio quality.

* Test your webcam and microphone before you start your call.

* Adjust your camera and microphone settings to your liking.

* Mute your microphone if you need to cough or sneeze.

* End the call if you need to step away for a moment.

WORKING WITH DOCUMENTS, SPREADSHEETS, AND PRESENTATIONS

Creating and editing documents with Google Docs

Here is a guide on how to create and edit documents with Google Docs:

Creating a New Document

To create a new document in Google Docs, follow these steps:

1. Open a web browser and go to docs.google.com.

2. Sign in to your Google Account.

3. Click on the "Create a new document" button.

4. A new blank document will open.

5. Start typing your document.

6. As you type, Google Docs will automatically save your work.

7. To save your work manually, click on the "File" menu and select "Save" or press Ctrl+S.

Editing a Document

To edit an existing document in Google Docs, follow these steps:

1. Open a web browser and go to docs.google.com.

2. Sign in to your Google Account.

3. Open the document you want to edit.

4. Start making changes to your document.

5. As you make changes, Google Docs will automatically save your work.

6. To save your work manually, click on the "File" menu and select "Save" or press Ctrl+S.

Formatting Text

To format text in Google Docs, you can use the following tools:

Font

Font size

Bold

Italic

Underline

Strikethrough

Color

Alignment

Bullets

Numbers

Indent

Line spacing

Adding Images

To add images to your Google Docs document, follow these steps:

1. Click on the "Insert" menu and select "Image".

2. Select the image you want to add from your computer.

3. Click on the "Open" button.

4. The image will be inserted into your document.

5. You can resize and move the image by clicking on it and dragging it to the desired location.

Adding Tables

To add tables to your Google Docs document, follow these steps:

1. Click on the "Insert" menu and select "Table".

2. Select the number of rows and columns you want in your table.

3. Click on the "Insert" button.

4. The table will be inserted into your document.

5. You can enter text into the cells of the table by clicking on them and typing.

6. You can resize the table by clicking on it and dragging the edges of the table.

Adding Links

To add links to your Google Docs document, follow these steps:

1. Highlight the text you want to add a link to.

2. Click on the "Insert" menu and select "Link".

3. Enter the URL of the link in the "Link to" field.

4. Click on the "OK" button.

5. The link will be added to the text.

6. To click on the link, press Ctrl+Click on the text.

Creating and editing spreadsheets with Google Sheets

Here is a guide on how to create and edit spreadsheets with Google Sheets:

Creating a new spreadsheet

To create a new spreadsheet in Google Sheets, follow these steps:

* Open a web browser and go to https://sheets.google.com/: https://sheets.google.com/.

* Sign in to your Google Account.

* Click on the "Create a new spreadsheet" button.

* A new blank spreadsheet will open.

* Start entering data into the cells of the spreadsheet.

* As you enter data, Google Sheets will automatically save your work.

* To save your work manually, click on the "File" menu and select "Save" or press Ctrl+S.

Editing an existing spreadsheet

To edit an existing spreadsheet in Google Sheets, follow these steps:

* Open a web browser and go to https://sheets.google.com/: https://sheets.google.com/.

* Sign in to your Google Account.

* Open the spreadsheet you want to edit.

* Start making changes to the spreadsheet.

* As you make changes, Google Sheets will automatically save your work.

* To save your work manually, click on the "File" menu and select "Save" or press Ctrl+S.

Formatting cells

To format cells in Google Sheets, you can use the following tools:

- Font

- Font size

- Bold

- Italic

- Underline

- Strikethrough

- Color

- Alignment

- Number format

- Borders

- Shading

Adding formulas

To add formulas to your Google Sheets spreadsheet, follow these steps:

* Click on the cell where you want to enter the formula.

* Type the formula into the cell.

* Press Enter.

* The result of the formula will be displayed in the cell.

Creating charts and graphs

To create charts and graphs in your Google Sheets spreadsheet, follow these steps:

* Select the data you want to chart or graph.

* Click on the "Insert" menu and select "Chart".

* The Chart Editor will open.

* Select the type of chart or graph you want to create.

* Customize the appearance of the chart or graph.

* Click on the "Insert" button.

* The chart or graph will be inserted into your spreadsheet.

Sharing and collaborating

To share and collaborate on your Google Sheets spreadsheet, follow these steps:

* Click on the "Share" button.

* Enter the email addresses of the people you want to share the spreadsheet with.

* Select the permissions you want to grant to each person.

* Click on the "Send" button.

* The people you shared the spreadsheet with will be able to view and edit the spreadsheet.

Creating and editing presentations with Google Slides

Here is a guide on how to create and edit presentations with Google Slides:

Creating a New Presentation

To create a new presentation in Google Slides, follow these steps:

1. Open a web browser and go to slides.google.com.

2. Sign in to your Google Account.

3. Click on the "Create a new presentation" button.

4. A new blank presentation will open.

5. Choose a theme for your presentation.

6. Add slides to your presentation by clicking on the "+" button next to the existing slides.

7. Add content to your slides by typing text, inserting images, or embedding videos.

8. As you add content, Google Slides will automatically save your work.

9. To save your work manually, click on the "File" menu and select "Save" or press Ctrl+S.

Editing an Existing Presentation

To edit an existing presentation in Google Slides, follow these steps:

1. Open a web browser and go to slides.google.com.

2. Sign in to your Google Account.

3. Open the presentation you want to edit.

4. Start making changes to the presentation.

5. As you make changes, Google Slides will automatically save your work.

6. To save your work manually, click on the "File" menu and select "Save" or press Ctrl+S.

Formatting Slides

To format slides in Google Slides, you can use the following tools:

Slide layout: You can choose from a variety of slide layouts, such as title slide, text slide, image slide, and video slide.

Background: You can choose a solid color, gradient, or image for the background of your slides.

Fonts: You can choose from a variety of fonts for the text in your slides.

Font size: You can change the font size of the text in your slides.

Bold: You can make the text in your slides bold.

Italic: You can make the text in your slides italic.

Underline: You can underline the text in your slides.

Strikethrough: You can strikethrough the text in your slides.

Colour: You can change the color of the text in your slides.

Alignment: You can change the alignment of the text in your slides.

Bullets: You can add bullets to your slides.

Numbers: You can add numbers to your slides.

Indent: You can indent the text in your slides.

Line spacing: You can change the line spacing of the text in your slides.

Adding Images and Videos

To add images and videos to your Google Slides presentation, follow these steps:

Images: Click on the "Insert" menu and select "Image". Select the image you want to add from your computer and click on the "Open" button.

Videos: Click on the "Insert" menu and select "Video". Paste the URL of the video you want to add into the "Video URL" field and click on the "Insert" button.

Animating Slides

To animate slides in your Google Slides presentation, follow these steps:

1. Select the slide you want to animate.

2. Click on the "Slide" menu and select "Animate".

3. In the "Animation pane," choose the animation you want to apply to the slide.

4. Click on the "Play" button to preview the animation.

5. Click on the "Save" button to save the animation.

Presenting Your Slides

To present your slides, follow these steps:

1. Open the presentation you want to present.

2. Click on the "Present" button.

3. Your slides will appear in full-screen mode.

4. To move to the next slide, click on the right arrow or press the right arrow key on your keyboard.

5. To move to the previous slide, click on the left arrow or press the left arrow key on your keyboard.

6. To end your presentation, press the Esc key on your keyboard.

STORING AND SHARING FILES WITH GOOGLE DRIVE

Uploading files to Google Drive

There are two ways to upload files to Google Drive:

Uploading files from your computer

1. Open a web browser and go to drive.google.com.

2. Sign in to your Google Account.

3. Click on the "New" button in the top left corner of the screen.

4. Select "File upload" from the menu.

5. Select the files you want to upload from your computer.

6. Click on the "Open" button.

7. The files will be uploaded to your Google Drive and will appear in the "My Drive" folder.

Dragging and dropping files into Google Drive

1. Open a web browser and go to drive.google.com.

2. Sign in to your Google Account.

3. Open the folder where you want to upload the files.

4. Drag and drop the files from your computer into the Google Drive folder.

5. The files will be uploaded to your Google Drive and will

appear in the folder you dragged them into.

Uploading files from your phone or tablet

1. Open the Google Drive app on your phone or tablet.

2. Tap on the "+" button in the bottom right corner of the screen.

3. Select "Upload" from the menu.

4. Select the files you want to upload from your phone or tablet.

5. Tap on the "Upload" button.

6. The files will be uploaded to your Google Drive and will appear in the "My Drive" folder.

Uploading folders to Google Drive

1. Open a web browser and go to drive.google.com.

2. Sign in to your Google Account.

3. Click on the "New" button in the top left corner of the screen.

4. Select "Folder upload" from the menu.

5. Select the folder you want to upload from your computer.

6. Click on the "Open" button.

7. The folder will be uploaded to your Google Drive and will appear in the "My Drive" folder.

Uploading folders from your phone or tablet

1. Open the Google Drive app on your phone or tablet.

2. Tap on the "+" button in the bottom right corner of the screen.

3. Select "Upload" from the menu.

4. Select the folder you want to upload from your phone or tablet.

5. Tap on the "Upload" button.

6. The folder will be uploaded to your Google Drive and will appear in the "My Drive" folder.

Sharing files with others

Sharing files with others allows you to grant access to specific individuals or groups to view, edit, or comment on your files. You can share files stored in various cloud storage services, such as Google Drive, Dropbox, and OneDrive.

Here are some steps on how to share files with others using Google Drive:

1. Open a web browser and go to drive.google.com.

2. Sign in to your Google Account.

3. Navigate to the file or folder you want to share.

4. Right-click on the file or folder and select the "Share" option.

5. In the "Share with people and groups" window, enter the email addresses of the people you

want to share the file or folder with.

6. Choose the permission level for each person you share the file or folder with. The options are:

Viewer: Can only view the file or folder.
Commenter: Can view and comment on the file or folder.
Editor: Can view, comment on, and edit the file or folder.

7. Click the "Send" button.

If you want to share the file or folder with a link, you can do the following:

1. In the "Share with people and groups" window, click the "Get link" option.

2. Choose the option for sharing the link:

Anyone with the link: Anyone who has the link can view the file or folder.

Specific people: Only the people you share the link with can view the file or folder.

3. Click the "Copy link" button.

4. Share the link with the people you want to give access to the file or folder.

Please note that sharing files with others can make them vulnerable to unauthorized access. It's important to only share files with people you trust and to make sure that your cloud storage account is secure.

Accessing files from anywhere

A key component of contemporary productivity and teamwork is the ability to access files from any location. Thanks to technological and cloud storage improvements, you may now access your data from any internet-connected device. You may work on papers, presentations, or other files from your house, workplace, or mobile device thanks to this flexibility.

The following are some popular methods for

accessing files from any location:

1. Cloud Storage Services: You may access your files from any device with an internet connection by using cloud storage services like Google Drive, Dropbox, and OneDrive, which act as a central repository for your information. Usually, these services provide synchronization and quick access through desktop and mobile apps.

2. Remote Desktop Access: You can access your computer

remotely from another device using remote desktop programs like TeamViewer and AnyDesk. This allows you to work on and access local machine files from any location in the world.

3. Servers for WebDAV: Through the use of a web browser and the WebDAV (Web Distributed Authoring and Versioning) protocol, data stored on a server can be accessed and managed. Using this way to access files from a personal or business server is especially helpful.

4. FTP (File Transfer Protocol): A common network protocol for file transfers across PCs on a TCP/IP network is FTP. Even while FTP isn't as safe as contemporary cloud-based options, it's nevertheless frequently used to access files on outdated servers or transmit big files.

5. VPNs (Virtual Private Networks): With the use of a virtual private network (VPN), you can access files and resources on the network just like if you were physically connected. This technique is very helpful for remote access to corporate files.

6. USB-Powered Storage Units: Flash drives and external hard drives are examples of USB storage devices that offer a portable solution for storing and accessing content from any location. To avoid data loss or damage, it's crucial to treat these devices carefully.

7. Offline Accessible Mobile Apps: You can work on files even when you don't have an internet connection thanks to the offline access feature of many mobile apps, including note-taking and document editors. Usually, these apps synchronize your modifications whenever you are online again.

8. File Sharing Links: You can create temporary links to share files with others using file sharing services like Send Anywhere and WeTransfer. You can use any internet-connected device to access these links.

9. Enclosed Email: Email attachments are still a popular means of sharing files with others, despite not being the best option for big files. Email attachments are accessible and downloadable from any device that has webmail or an email client installed.

10. Platforms for Social Media: There are social networking services, like Facebook and Google Drive, that let you share files directly with other users. Sharing files with individuals you already have connections with on social media is especially easy with this strategy.

Always put security first while gaining remote access to files. Make sure to activate two-factor authentication, create secure passwords, and exercise caution when using third-party websites and services to access your assets.

TROUBLESHOOTING COMMON PROBLEMS

What to do if you forget your password

Forgetting passwords can happen to anyone at any time. If you've forgotten your password, don't panic. There are usually steps you can take to recover your account and access your information.

Here are some general tips for dealing with a forgotten password:

1. Remain calm: Panicking will not help you remember your password. Take a few deep breaths and try to think clearly.

2. Check for saved passwords: If you have a password manager or your web browser saves passwords, check there first. You may find your password saved for the account you're trying to access.

3. Look for password hints: Many websites and services provide password hints to help you jog your memory. These hints may be related to personal information, such as your birthday, hometown, or favorite pet.

4. Try common passwords: If you tend to use common passwords, try some of your most frequently used passwords. You may have simply forgotten which one you used for this particular account.

5. Use password recovery tools: Most websites and services offer password recovery tools. These tools will typically send you a link or email with instructions on how to reset your password.

6. **Contact customer support:** If you've tried all the above and still can't remember your password, contact the customer support for the website or service you need to access. They may be able to help you reset your password or provide other assistance.

Here are some specific steps you can take for different types of accounts:

Email accounts:

1. Check your email provider's password recovery page.

2. Enter the email address you want to recover the password for.

3. Select the option to reset your password using a security question or phone number associated with your account.

4. Follow the instructions provided to reset your password.

Social media accounts:

1. Go to the social media platform's password recovery page.

2. Enter the email address or phone number associated with your account.

3. Select the option to reset your password using a security question or email verification.

4. Follow the instructions provided to reset your password.

Online banking accounts:

1. Go to your bank's website or mobile app.

2. Click on the "Forgot Password" or "Reset Password" link.

3. Enter your email address or account number associated with your account.

4. Select the option to reset your password using a security question or email verification.

5. Follow the instructions provided to reset your password.

If you're still having trouble remembering your password, you may need to contact the customer support for the specific account you're trying to access. They may be able to provide additional assistance or help you create a new password.

In general, it's a good idea to create strong passwords that you can remember and to use different passwords for different accounts. You should also consider using a password manager to help you keep track of your passwords.

what to do if your Chromebook is not working properly

There are several things you can do if your Chromebook is not working properly. Here are a few suggestions:

Check for updates: Make sure your Chromebook is up to date with the latest software. Outdated software can cause a variety of problems, so it's important to keep your system up-to-date. To check for updates, click the time in the bottom right corner of the screen and then select the gear icon. Click "About Chrome OS" and then click "Check for updates." If there are any updates available, Chrome OS will download and install them.

Restart your Chromebook: Sometimes, a simple restart can fix minor problems. To restart your Chromebook, click the time in the bottom right corner of the screen and then select the power icon. Click "Restart."

Reset your Chromebook: If restarting your Chromebook doesn't fix the problem, you can try resetting it to factory settings. This will erase all of your data and settings, so make sure you have a backup before you proceed. To reset your Chromebook, click the time in the bottom right corner of the screen and then select the gear icon. Click "About Chrome OS" and then click "Powerwash." Follow the instructions on the screen to reset your Chromebook.

Hard refresh: If you're having problems with a specific website or web page, you can try a hard refresh. To do this, press Ctrl + Shift + R on your keyboard. This will clear your browser's cache and reload the page from the server.

Disable extensions: If you've recently installed any new extensions, try disabling them to see if they're causing the problem. To disable an extension, click the three dots in the top right corner of the Chrome window and then select "More tools" and "Extensions."

Click the toggle switch next to an extension to disable it.

Powerwash: If all else fails, you can try powerwashing your Chromebook. This will erase all of your data and settings, so make sure you have a backup before you proceed. To powerwash your Chromebook, click the time in the bottom right corner of the screen and then select the power icon. Click "Restart." When your Chromebook restarts, press and hold the Esc, Ctrl, and Alt keys together, and then press the Power button. Follow the instructions on the screen to powerwash your Chromebook.

If you've tried all of these suggestions and your Chromebook is still not working properly, you may need to contact Google support for further assistance.

Here are some additional tips for keeping your Chromebook running smoothly:

Close unused tabs and windows: This will free up

memory and help your Chromebook run faster.

Delete old files and unused apps: This will free up storage space and help your Chromebook run more efficiently.

Keep your Chromebook clean: Dust and debris can clog your Chromebook's vents and fan, which can cause overheating and other problems.

Avoid using your Chromebook in extreme temperatures: Don't leave your Chromebook in direct sunlight or in a hot car.

Be careful what you download: Only download files from trusted sources to avoid malware and viruses.

Keep your Chromebook up to date: Make sure your Chromebook is up to date with the latest software to fix bugs and security vulnerabilities.

By following these tips, you can help keep your Chromebook running smoothly and prevent problems from occurring in the first place.

Where to find additional help

If you're still having trouble, you can find additional help from a variety of sources:

Google support: Google offers a variety of support resources for Chromebook users, including online help articles, troubleshooting guides, and a community forum. You can find Google support here: [https://support.google.com/ch

romebook/?hl=en](https://supp
ort.google.com/chromebook/?hl
=en)

Manufacturer support: If
you purchased your
Chromebook from a specific
manufacturer, you can also
contact their customer support
for assistance. They may be able
to provide more specific
troubleshooting steps for your
Chromebook model.

**Online forums and
communities**: There are many
online forums and communities
where Chromebook users can

ask for help and share solutions to common problems. A popular forum for Chromebook users is Chromebook Central: https://www.androidcentral.com/chromebooks-laptops

Local repair shops: If you're not comfortable troubleshooting your Chromebook yourself, you can take it to a local computer repair shop. They will be able to diagnose the problem and fix it for you.

www.ingramcontent.com/pod-product-compliance
Lightning Source LLC
La Vergne TN
LVHW051338050326
832903LV00031B/3614

Chapter 1: A New AI Partner in the Team

Chapter 1: A New AI Partner in the Team

The conference room was quiet as Bob powered up his laptop, projecting a blank screen onto the wall. His team—Alex, Jordan, Pat, and Riley—sat around the table, each of them looking curious yet slightly apprehensive. They knew today's meeting would bring something different. It wasn't another project kickoff or a review of the latest sprint. This meeting was about change, a new way of working, and possibly a new perspective on software development.

"Alright, everyone," Bob began, his tone warm but firm. "Today, we're bringing in a new team member—an AI assistant designed to help us tackle the technical challenges of software development. This AI is different from what we've used in the past, and it's here to support, not replace, the work we do."

The projector screen came to life with a simple interface that displayed the name "Codey." Bob watched as the team members exchanged glances, their reactions ranging from intrigue to skepticism.

"This is Codey," he said, gesturing to the screen. "Think of Codey as an AI-powered junior developer with a specialized focus on our work. Codey can help streamline coding tasks, suggest debugging strategies, generate test cases, and even provide architectural insights. It's like having a highly capable assistant that doesn't tire, doesn't need breaks, and can analyze code at a remarkable speed."

Jordan leaned forward, her eyes alight with curiosity. "So, Codey's going to be working with us on everything from testing to design?"

Bob nodded. "That's right. But Codey's role will evolve based on how we decide to use it. It's a flexible tool, designed to help us be more efficient. However, it's still a tool. We're the ones in charge, and our expertise is still what guides every project."

Initial Reactions and Perspectives

The team's responses to Codey varied. Jordan seemed excited about the possibilities, already imagining ways the AI could save time and help her learn new techniques. Pat, with his strategic eye for architecture, was intrigued but cautious, recognizing that Codey might offer suggestions, yet only they could judge the best path forward. Alex folded his arms, wearing his skepticism plainly. He'd seen tools come and go, and while he was open-minded, he wasn't easily convinced. Riley, ever diligent and precise, took a thoughtful approach, already considering how AI could improve her QA process but also aware of the potential pitfalls.

"Let's be clear," Bob continued, addressing the room. "Codey is here to enhance what we do, not to replace our roles or diminish our impact. Think of it as a partner that will help us tackle the routine and repetitive tasks, freeing up more of our time for strategic, high-value work."

Codey's First Task: Basic Coding Assistance

To give the team a firsthand look at Codey's capabilities, Bob pulled up a small, unfinished coding task and invited Codey to analyze it. In seconds, Codey highlighted a few suggested improvements, ranging from syntax adjustments to minor optimizations that could reduce processing time.

Jordan's eyes widened. "That was fast! It would have taken me a while to catch all of those details."

Bob smiled. "Exactly. Codey's processing power allows it to scan through code quickly and identify opportunities for improvement. However, these are just suggestions. It's still up to us to determine if they're relevant."

Alex leaned in, skeptical but intrigued. "Sure, it's fast, but what about more complex logic? Can it handle nuances, or is it just scanning for simple errors?"

"Good question," Bob replied. "Codey can handle patterns and make suggestions, but it doesn't understand our intent. It won't always get the nuances right, which is why your judgment is essential. Codey's here to catch the things we might overlook but won't replace the problem-solving and decision-making that only we can provide."

Setting Expectations and Initial Guidelines

Bob handed out a list of preliminary guidelines, underscoring how they'd incorporate Codey without losing control over their work.

- **Use Codey for Routine Tasks**: Begin with Codey handling repetitive coding, initial code review, and debugging suggestions.

- **Maintain Human Oversight**: Always validate Codey's suggestions, especially when they affect complex code logic.

- **Document AI Interactions**: Track where Codey was most helpful and where it needed human correction, so they could refine their approach.

- **Encourage Experimentation**: Each team member was encouraged to use Codey in different areas and share their experiences.

"Consider this the start of an ongoing experiment," Bob said. "We'll learn as we go, and Codey will evolve with us. We don't expect perfection from it, and we shouldn't expect it from ourselves, either. Let's see where this takes us."

As the team dispersed, Bob felt a mixture of optimism and anticipation. Codey represented an exciting step forward, but he knew this was only the beginning of their journey. How they navigated the balance between AI and human expertise would define their success.

Alex's Notebook

- Codey's speed is impressive, but I'm still cautious about relying too heavily on it.

- Human oversight will be critical; AI can't capture our project's unique needs.

- Documenting our experiences with Codey is a good idea—we'll see where it adds real value.

- I'm curious but reserved; we'll see if this AI is more than just a tool.

- The key will be using Codey for efficiency without compromising quality.

Jordan's Notebook

- Codey seems like an amazing resource—I can already see ways to save time.

- Learning from Codey's suggestions might help me grow as a developer.

- I'll focus on tracking where Codey adds the most value to see patterns.

- Excited to work with an AI that can offer coding insights at lightning speed.

- Looking forward to experimenting with Codey in testing and debugging.

Pat's Notebook

- Codey could be useful in initial design and architecture suggestions.

- The idea of AI for routine tasks is appealing, freeing up time for high-level work.

- We need to document Codey's outputs to refine its role over time.

- AI offers a unique perspective, but our experience is what will make the difference.

- I'm cautiously optimistic—Codey could be a valuable partner in efficiency.

Riley's Notebook

- Codey has potential, especially in handling repetitive testing tasks.

- Validating AI outputs will be crucial to avoid missed issues.

- Documenting AI interactions will be key for tracking long-term success.

- Codey can assist in my work, but human judgment will be vital for quality assurance.

- Looking forward to seeing how Codey can streamline our testing workflow.

Bob's Notebook

- Excited to see how the team integrates Codey and finds value in AI assistance.

- Documentation of AI insights will help us assess Codey's evolving role.

- Encouraging a balanced approach—AI as an assistant, with humans as decision-makers.

- Experimentation and adaptability will be our strengths in this journey.

- Confident that Codey can enhance our workflows when used thoughtfully.

Practical Advice

- Use AI tools for repetitive coding tasks but maintain human oversight.

- Track and document AI outputs to understand its impact on workflow efficiency.
- Balance AI suggestions with human judgment, focusing on quality.
- Encourage experimentation to find where AI provides the most value.
- Recognize that AI is an assistant, not a replacement, for experienced developers.

Implementation

- Start by integrating AI in routine coding tasks and initial reviews.
- Establish protocols for reviewing and validating AI-generated outputs.
- Document experiences with AI to track areas of effectiveness and improvement.
- Encourage team experimentation with AI in various development areas.
- Regularly review the balance between AI and manual coding efforts.

Real-World Insight

In the tech industry, AI tools are increasingly used to support software development by automating repetitive tasks and speeding up processes. Companies leverage AI for code review, testing, and debugging, freeing developers to focus on higher-level decisions. While AI can enhance productivity, the most effective results come from combining AI assistance with skilled human oversight.

Pitfalls to Avoid

- Over-relying on AI for complex coding decisions without validation.
- Neglecting documentation of AI outputs, missing valuable insights.
- Allowing AI suggestions to compromise team quality standards.
- Assuming AI can replace human expertise in nuanced coding tasks.

- Failing to balance AI speed with careful review for long-term reliability.

Self-Assessment

- How comfortable am I with using AI to assist in coding tasks?
- What areas of development can AI improve in our workflow?
- How can I ensure AI outputs align with project requirements?
- What strategies can I use to validate AI suggestions?
- How can I use AI to support my growth as a developer?

Self-Reflection

- Reflect on initial thoughts about using AI—have they changed?
- How do you see AI fitting into your development workflow going forward?
- Are there aspects of coding where human oversight feels essential? Why?
- How can AI assist you in becoming a more efficient developer?
- What steps can you take to ensure a balanced approach with AI in coding?

Chapter 2: Streamlining Code Writing – Codey's First Assist

Chapter 2: Streamlining Code Writing – Codey's First Assist

As the team settled into the rhythm of the week, Bob decided it was time to give Codey its first official task. After the initial excitement of introducing the AI to the team, he knew that diving into a hands-on assignment would be the best way to uncover its strengths and limitations. Today's focus was code writing—a central part of their daily work and an ideal area to test Codey's capabilities.

Bob gathered everyone around the shared screen. "Today, we're going to see how Codey can help us streamline code writing. Codey's designed to speed up routine coding tasks, offering us suggestions for improved syntax, structure, and even code snippets."

Jordan's enthusiasm was clear as she spoke up. "So, Codey will help us write the code directly?"

"In a way," Bob replied. "Codey can suggest code blocks and identify places where we might optimize, but it's still up to us to make final decisions. Think of it as an extra pair of hands that never tires."

Alex, ever the skeptic, raised a brow. "Is it really helping, though, or is it just following patterns? Real coding is more than just syntax—it's problem-solving."

"You're right, Alex," Bob acknowledged. "Codey doesn't understand our intent. It's not going to replace the critical thinking behind coding. But it can accelerate some of the more routine aspects, so we can focus on the parts that require creativity and logic."

Codey's First Coding Task

To get a feel for how Codey could assist in coding, Bob pulled up a new feature they'd been discussing—a complex function designed to manage and process user inputs. He invited Codey to review the initial code and provide suggestions.

Within moments, Codey displayed its first round of feedback:

- **Syntax Optimization**: Codey suggested minor adjustments in the syntax for better readability and efficiency.

- **Code Simplification**: It proposed combining redundant lines to streamline the function.

- **Error Prevention**: Codey flagged a few spots where variable declarations could be improved to avoid potential errors.

Jordan leaned forward, clearly impressed. "It's like having an instant second opinion. This would save so much time on the repetitive checks."

Bob nodded. "Exactly. Codey's designed to help with these basics, giving us a jumpstart so we can focus on refining the logic."

Pat reviewed the suggestions with a critical eye. "It's a good start, but we still need to think about edge cases and the broader context. Codey doesn't account for how this code might interact with other parts of the project."

"True," Bob agreed. "That's why this process is still collaborative. Codey gives us options, but we're the ones who decide if they're viable."

Encouraging Experimentation

With Codey's suggestions as a starting point, Bob encouraged the team to experiment. Jordan took the lead, applying some of Codey's syntax improvements and seeing immediate results in readability. Meanwhile, Pat tested the AI's suggestions in a sandbox environment, ensuring they didn't introduce unexpected issues.

Alex observed, quietly impressed despite himself. "Alright, maybe there's some value here. Codey seems to handle the tedious bits well."

Riley joined in, "It's like having a tool that catches the small stuff so we can focus on the bigger issues. But I think it'll be important to document each change we make with Codey's input. If we need to troubleshoot later, we'll know what came from AI."

Bob smiled. "Good point, Riley. Let's track Codey's contributions and build a habit of validating them. This way, we can measure its impact on our workflow and decide where it's truly helpful."

Initial Guidelines for Code Writing with AI

As the team wrapped up their session, Bob distributed some guidelines for using Codey in their code writing processes:

- **Use AI for Routine Suggestions**: Allow Codey to handle syntax adjustments, minor optimizations, and repetitive tasks.

- **Maintain Contextual Awareness**: AI provides suggestions without understanding project goals. Ensure every change aligns with the broader objectives.

- **Document AI Contributions**: Keep track of Codey's recommendations and note any adjustments made, for transparency and troubleshooting.

- **Balance AI and Manual Input**: Use Codey's efficiency to accelerate simpler tasks, saving energy for more complex coding decisions.

- **Encourage Testing and Reflection**: Apply Codey's suggestions in isolated environments first, and reflect on the outcomes before committing to final versions.

Bob concluded, "This is just the beginning. As we get more familiar with Codey, we'll refine how we use it. Remember, the goal is to enhance our productivity without sacrificing the quality of our work."

The team dispersed, feeling a growing sense of excitement about the potential Codey brought to their workflow. Each of them knew that using AI for coding was uncharted territory, but they were ready to navigate it together.

Alex's Notebook

- Codey seems efficient with basic code checks, but I'm still cautious.
- Documenting AI contributions will help track any future issues.
- We need to be careful not to let AI remove the human element in coding.
- I'm seeing potential but will watch closely for any over-reliance.
- This is just a tool—it's still up to us to make smart decisions.

Jordan's Notebook

- Codey makes code writing faster by catching small details.
- It's a great tool for learning; I'm picking up on its suggestions.
- Documenting AI suggestions will help us understand where it adds value.
- Excited to see how Codey improves routine tasks.
- This partnership feels promising for saving time.

Pat's Notebook

- AI can improve our efficiency in coding, but context is essential.
- Documenting AI-driven changes is key to transparent coding.

- Codey's syntax improvements are helpful but require our oversight.
- I'm intrigued by how this will scale with more complex functions.
- AI can handle some tedious tasks, allowing us to focus on design.

Riley's Notebook

- Codey speeds up coding but needs close validation.
- Documenting AI outputs is essential for tracking its effectiveness.
- Excited to see how AI assists in repetitive code-writing tasks.
- Using AI cautiously ensures quality remains our top priority.
- Optimistic but careful about relying on AI in daily work.

Bob's Notebook

- Codey's initial input shows promise, but human oversight is key.
- Documentation of AI suggestions is crucial to refining our process.
- Encouraging the team to balance AI efficiency with quality standards.
- Experimentation and adaptation will help us find Codey's best uses.
- Confident that Codey can streamline tasks without replacing human skills.

Practical Advice

- Use AI to assist with routine code-writing tasks, such as syntax adjustments and optimizations.
- Track AI-driven changes to assess their impact and support troubleshooting.
- Balance AI inputs with manual validation to ensure quality.
- Test AI suggestions in isolated environments to gauge effectiveness.

- Encourage experimentation to learn where AI provides the most value.

Implementation

- Begin by using AI for routine coding checks and optimizations.
- Document AI outputs and track adjustments for transparency.
- Apply AI suggestions cautiously, ensuring they align with project needs.
- Experiment with AI-driven syntax improvements to gauge efficiency.
- Regularly review the balance between AI and manual coding efforts.

Real-World Insight

Many tech companies are integrating AI to assist with code writing, using tools like GitHub Copilot to speed up syntax checks, identify common errors, and optimize code. By automating repetitive tasks, these tools free up developers to focus on complex logic and project-specific goals. However, successful integration depends on balancing AI assistance with human expertise.

Pitfalls to Avoid

- Relying on AI for complex coding decisions without validation.
- Failing to document AI-driven changes, losing context for future debugging.
- Allowing AI to replace essential human judgment in code logic.
- Ignoring the need for project-specific context in AI recommendations.
- Neglecting to test AI-suggested changes in safe environments.

Self-Assessment

- How comfortable am I with using AI for code writing assistance?
- What types of code-writing tasks can AI improve in my workflow?

- How can I ensure AI outputs align with our project goals?

- What strategies can I use to validate AI suggestions effectively?

- How can AI support my growth as a developer?

Self-Reflection

- Reflect on initial thoughts about AI in code writing—have they changed?

- How do you see AI fitting into your code-writing workflow moving forward?

- Are there aspects of coding where human oversight is crucial? Why?

- How can AI assist you in becoming a more efficient coder?

- What steps can you take to ensure a balanced approach with AI in coding?

Chapter 3: Ideation and Architecture – Designing with Codey

Chapter 3: Ideation and Architecture – Designing with Codey

The conference room felt like the team's workshop, a creative space where they brainstormed, sketched ideas, and hashed out the high-level architecture of their projects. Today, though, Bob wanted to add something new to their design sessions—Codey.

"Alright, everyone," Bob began, motioning to the screen. "We've seen how Codey can help with coding and syntax checks. Now, we're going to see if it can support us in the design phase by generating ideas for system architecture and suggesting options for optimization."

Pat, the team's architect, leaned in, intrigued. "You're saying Codey can offer design input, too?"

"Exactly," Bob replied. "Codey won't give us finished designs, but it can highlight patterns, suggest modular structures, and help us brainstorm architectural options we might not think of right away."

Jordan looked excited. "This could save so much time on brainstorming and testing different structures."

Bob nodded. "That's the goal. Codey can act as a design assistant, proposing ideas we might refine or build upon. Think of it as a tool for ideation, helping us to see the bigger picture."

Codey's First Architecture Suggestions

Bob pulled up the outline of a new project—a user management system with multiple interfaces and a complex backend. With a few commands, he invited Codey to analyze the project requirements and propose architectural options.

Within moments, Codey displayed several ideas:

- **Modular Design**: Codey recommended breaking down the system into smaller, independent modules to facilitate updates and scalability.

- **Microservices Architecture**: For better performance and easier maintenance, Codey suggested a microservices approach, dividing the system into standalone services that could be managed independently.

- **Database Indexing Suggestions**: Codey highlighted the benefits of specific indexing in the database, which could improve query efficiency in user data retrieval.

Pat examined Codey's suggestions. "It's not bad—these are solid foundational ideas. The microservices approach could give us flexibility, especially if the user management system grows."

"Agreed," Bob said. "And remember, these are just starting points. Codey doesn't account for our project's unique goals, so it's up to us to determine what fits best."

Balancing AI Suggestions with Practical Needs

With Codey's insights as a foundation, the team began sketching out potential architectures. Pat took the lead, incorporating Codey's modular and microservices ideas into a rough blueprint. However, as they dove deeper, they noticed that some of Codey's suggestions were too resource-intensive for their current budget.

"This indexing idea is useful for performance, but we'd have to balance the storage costs," Riley pointed out. "It's helpful, but we'll need to customize it to our actual constraints."

Jordan added, "Codey's modular approach is good, but some modules might overlap too much. We could simplify a few areas to save on processing."

Bob encouraged the team to refine Codey's suggestions, shaping them to meet their specific needs. "That's the strength of combining AI and human insight. Codey gives us the starting points, but we make the decisions."

Guidelines for AI in Architectural Design

After wrapping up the initial design session, Bob laid out guidelines to help the team use Codey more effectively in future architectural planning.

- **Use AI for Foundational Suggestions**: Codey can propose structural frameworks, but final designs should be refined by the team.

- **Maintain Project-Specific Focus**: Ensure that every AI suggestion aligns with project goals, resources, and constraints.

- **Document AI-Driven Ideas**: Track AI-generated architecture concepts and note where adjustments are made for transparency.

- **Balance AI Efficiency with Practicality**: AI may prioritize efficiency over feasibility; adjust recommendations to match the project's practical needs.

- **Encourage Collaborative Ideation**: Use AI suggestions as a base, then work together to enhance and adapt the ideas.

Bob concluded, "Codey is like a brainstorming partner—use its suggestions to jumpstart our thinking, but we're still in charge of shaping the final structure. This balance is where AI can really enhance our process."

21

As they left the meeting, the team felt a renewed sense of direction. Codey was proving to be a valuable assistant, one that gave them more to think about and build upon. They were beginning to see AI not as a replacement but as a catalyst for their creativity.

Alex's Notebook

- Codey's foundational suggestions speed up the initial design process.

- Important to remember that AI doesn't fully grasp project constraints.

- Documenting AI ideas helps track which suggestions we adapt or change.

- Balancing efficiency and practicality is key in architectural design.

- AI is a helpful brainstorming tool, but human insight is crucial.

Jordan's Notebook

- Codey's ideas provide a good starting point for architecture discussions.

- Learning to refine AI suggestions helps me understand design choices.

- Documenting our adaptations of AI ideas shows where AI adds value.

- Excited about how AI can assist with complex structural decisions.

- This partnership enhances brainstorming but keeps us in control.

Pat's Notebook

- Codey's modular and microservices suggestions were valuable options.

- Balancing AI recommendations with project-specific needs is essential.

- Documentation of AI-driven design ideas is key to refining our approach.

- AI offers structural insight but requires human oversight.

- This collaborative process feels more efficient without losing depth.

Riley's Notebook

- Codey's design suggestions are useful but need verification.
- Tracking AI-suggested structures helps ensure quality in the final product.
- Combining AI with human oversight supports well-rounded architecture.
- AI assists with complex tasks, but we ensure practical constraints.
- Optimistic about using AI in planning, provided we keep oversight.

Bob's Notebook

- Codey provides a fast, efficient foundation for brainstorming.
- Documenting AI-driven ideas is crucial for transparency and tracking.
- Encouraging the team to balance AI's efficiency with practical constraints.
- Architecture decisions need human context to meet project goals.
- Confident that AI can enhance ideation without replacing human insight.

Practical Advice

- Use AI tools to support foundational brainstorming and structural design.
- Always review AI-driven ideas to ensure alignment with project needs.
- Track AI-suggested structures and note any adaptations made by the team.
- Balance AI-driven efficiency with practical considerations in design.
- Encourage collaborative ideation to refine and customize AI suggestions.

Implementation

- Begin by using AI for initial structural suggestions in project planning.
- Establish protocols for reviewing and adapting AI-driven architectural ideas.

- Document AI suggestions and track any modifications for clarity.

- Use AI insights as a base to streamline ideation and design efficiency.

- Regularly assess the balance between AI-generated and team-generated designs.

Real-World Insight

Companies increasingly leverage AI to support the architectural design phase, with tools that analyze requirements and propose structural frameworks. AI-driven suggestions can speed up the ideation process, especially in complex systems, but the final architecture must always align with business goals, resource availability, and scalability needs. Successful implementations strike a balance between AI insights and human refinement.

Pitfalls to Avoid

- Over-relying on AI for architectural decisions without customization.

- Implementing AI-driven structures without considering project constraints.

- Failing to document AI-driven ideas, losing transparency and traceability.

- Allowing AI's efficiency focus to overshadow practical feasibility.

- Neglecting the importance of human oversight in architectural design.

Self-Assessment

- How comfortable am I with using AI for architectural brainstorming?

- What structural suggestions can AI improve in our design process?

- How can I ensure AI-driven designs align with our project constraints?

- What strategies can I use to validate AI suggestions in architecture?

- How can AI support my growth as a designer or developer?

Self-Reflection

- Reflect on initial thoughts about AI in design—have they evolved?

- How do you see AI fitting into your architectural workflow going forward?

- Are there aspects of design where human oversight feels essential? Why?

- How can AI assist you in becoming more effective in structural planning?

- What steps can you take to ensure a balanced approach with AI in design?

Chapter 4: Automation and Testing – Finding Efficiency with AI

Chapter 4: Automation and Testing – Finding Efficiency with AI

Riley sat at her workstation, reviewing a long list of test cases. As the team's quality assurance expert, she knew the importance of rigorous testing, but the sheer volume of repetitive checks could be overwhelming. Today, however, Bob had a new idea. "Let's see how Codey can assist us with automated testing," he announced, drawing everyone's attention.

Bob continued, "Testing is one of the most time-consuming parts of our workflow, and with Codey, we may be able to free up more of your time, Riley, for the more complex analysis while letting AI handle the routine checks."

Riley raised a brow, intrigued. "Automated testing sounds promising. But can Codey really understand the nuances of our test cases?"

Bob nodded thoughtfully. "That's a valid point. Codey can't replace your expertise, Riley, but it can help with the simpler, repetitive tasks, giving us a solid foundation that you can build upon."

Codey's First Pass at Automated Testing

To test Codey's capabilities, Bob pulled up the latest module the team was working on—a user input form with multiple validation points. He instructed Codey to generate a set of automated test cases.

Within seconds, Codey displayed an array of tests:

- **Basic Functionality Testing**: Codey proposed tests to verify that each field in the form functioned as intended.

- **Edge Case Detection**: Codey suggested input limits to identify potential vulnerabilities or unexpected behaviors.

- **Load Testing**: It recommended a series of stress tests to ensure the form could handle high volumes of input simultaneously.

Jordan leaned in, clearly impressed. "It's like Codey's thought of every possible scenario!"

Riley scanned the test cases, cautiously optimistic. "These are solid, but we'll need to validate them. Testing isn't just about catching bugs; it's about ensuring every aspect works together as intended."

"Exactly," Bob agreed. "Think of Codey as a tool that handles the heavy lifting, so you can focus on analyzing and refining the results."

Balancing AI-Driven Testing with Quality Control

Chapter 4: Automation and Testing – Finding Efficiency with AI

As the team incorporated Codey's test cases, they encountered both benefits and limitations. Codey's automation accelerated basic checks, but certain aspects, like user experience flows and specific integration points, required Riley's careful review and adjustment.

"Codey's coverage is broad," Pat observed, "but we still need to go deeper into the areas that require our domain knowledge."

Riley nodded. "That's why it's important to document where Codey's suggestions help and where they fall short. Testing isn't just about quantity—it's about quality and relevance."

Alex raised a question. "How do we know when to trust Codey's test cases and when we need to step in for a closer look?"

Bob replied, "That's why we document and evaluate. The goal is to use Codey for routine checks while you focus on critical areas. Think of it as a way to free up resources without losing control over quality."

Guidelines for AI-Assisted Testing

After reviewing Codey's contributions, Bob outlined best practices for integrating AI into their testing processes effectively:

- **Leverage AI for Repetitive Tasks**: Use Codey to automate standard test cases and regression testing, reserving human focus for complex scenarios.

- **Maintain Human Oversight**: Review and validate all AI-generated test cases, ensuring alignment with project requirements.

- **Focus on High-Risk Areas**: Let Codey handle routine checks, but prioritize manual testing for areas with higher potential impact.

- **Document AI Contributions**: Track where Codey was effective and where additional refinement was necessary to guide future use.

- **Balance Automation with Manual Testing**: Combine AI and human testing to achieve comprehensive quality assurance.

"We've seen that Codey can be a powerful asset," Bob concluded. "But testing still requires a balance. Let's use AI to enhance our process without compromising our standards."

The team left the meeting, each feeling a mix of excitement and caution. Codey was proving to be a valuable partner in speeding up routine tasks, but they knew their expertise was still the foundation of quality.

Alex's Notebook

- Codey is helpful for broad coverage, but human judgment is essential.

- Documenting AI-driven tests helps track where it's effective and where it's not.

- Balancing automated and manual testing ensures comprehensive coverage.

- Testing quality remains the team's responsibility, even with AI.

- AI in testing is promising, but we need to stay vigilant.

Jordan's Notebook

- Codey's test suggestions speed up repetitive checks, saving time.

- Learning from Codey's approach helps expand my own testing perspective.

- Documentation of AI contributions is helpful for refining future testing.

- AI is a great support tool but doesn't replace quality-focused testing.

- Excited to see how AI can continue to improve testing workflows.

Pat's Notebook

- Codey's broad testing coverage complements our detailed manual testing.

- Balancing automation with human oversight is critical for quality.

- Documenting AI contributions keeps testing transparent and effective.

- Optimistic about how AI can improve testing efficiency without sacrificing quality.

- This approach enhances our workflow but requires careful oversight.

Riley's Notebook

- Codey supports efficiency in repetitive tests but requires close validation.

- Maintaining documentation of AI-driven tests aids in quality assurance.

- AI can handle routine checks, but we ensure high-risk areas are well-tested.

- Testing still requires expertise to ensure standards are met.

- Cautiously optimistic about AI's role in the QA process.

Bob's Notebook

- AI-driven testing improves efficiency but requires vigilant oversight.

- Documenting AI's role in testing is crucial for transparency and quality.

- Encouraging the team to balance AI with manual efforts in QA.

- Confident that AI can complement our testing when used thoughtfully.

- The team's expertise is still the foundation of our testing standards.

Practical Advice

- Use AI tools to automate repetitive testing tasks and free up human resources.

- Always validate AI-generated test cases to ensure they align with quality standards.

- Track AI-driven tests and document any adjustments to refine future testing.

- Focus manual efforts on high-risk areas, letting AI handle routine checks.

- Balance automated and manual testing to maintain comprehensive coverage.

Implementation

- Start by integrating AI for routine and regression testing tasks.

- Establish guidelines for reviewing and validating AI-generated test cases.

- Document outcomes of AI-driven testing to guide future improvements.

- Allocate time saved through AI for manual testing in critical areas.

- Regularly assess the balance between automated and human-driven testing.

Real-World Insight

Many software development teams incorporate AI to assist with automated testing, using tools like Testim, Applitools, and others to streamline repetitive test cases and regression tests. These tools enable developers to focus on high-priority areas, improving both efficiency and coverage. However, successful implementations balance automation with human oversight to ensure quality remains at the forefront.

Pitfalls to Avoid

- Relying solely on AI for testing without manual validation.

- Failing to document AI-driven tests, which may lead to gaps in quality control.

- Allowing AI to overshadow the importance of critical thinking in QA.

- Overlooking context-specific areas that require human expertise.

- Ignoring the need for balanced coverage between automated and manual tests.

Self-Assessment

- How comfortable am I with using AI for automated testing?

- In which areas can AI improve our testing efficiency?

- How can I ensure AI-generated test cases align with project goals?

- What strategies can I use to validate AI suggestions effectively?

- How can AI support my role in maintaining high standards in QA?

Self-Reflection

- Reflect on initial thoughts about AI in testing—have they evolved?

- How do you see AI fitting into your testing workflow moving forward?

- Are there aspects of testing where human oversight is crucial? Why?

- How can AI assist you in becoming a more efficient tester?

- What steps can you take to ensure a balanced approach with AI in QA?

Chapter 5: Debugging with AI – Codey's Role in Problem Solving

Chapter 5: Debugging with AI – Codey's Role in Problem Solving

The development room was quiet as the team tackled one of their most challenging tasks: debugging. Bugs could be elusive, hiding deep within complex code, and the time spent finding them often strained their project timelines. Today, Bob had called a meeting to introduce Codey's potential role in the debugging process.

"Alright, team," Bob began, addressing the group. "Debugging is one of the most time-consuming parts of development, but with Codey's help, we might be able to streamline it. Codey can analyze code patterns and point out areas where bugs are likely to occur, giving us a head start."

Riley looked intrigued. "So Codey will actually help us pinpoint the problem areas?"

Bob nodded. "That's the idea. Codey can't fully understand the nuances of our code, but it can scan the entire codebase in seconds, highlighting patterns and issues that may take us hours to identify."

Codey's First Debugging Session

To put Codey to the test, Bob pulled up a problematic section of their current project—a complex function with multiple nested conditions and loops that had been throwing errors intermittently. He asked Codey to analyze the code and identify any potential issues.

In moments, Codey flagged several lines as "high-likelihood error zones" and suggested a few possible causes:

- **Variable Scope Issues**: Codey identified variables that could potentially conflict due to scope limitations.

- **Logic Flow Gaps**: It highlighted certain conditional blocks where edge cases might not be fully handled.

- **Memory Leaks**: Codey suggested areas where memory management could be optimized, potentially resolving some instability.

Pat, who had been reviewing Codey's analysis, raised an eyebrow. "These are good insights. Normally, I'd spend a lot of time narrowing down these exact points."

Jordan chimed in, "It's like Codey's giving us a roadmap. But how do we know if these are actual issues or just possibilities?"

Chapter 5: Debugging with AI – Codey's Role in Problem Solving

"Good question," Bob replied. "Codey's suggestions are meant to help us focus our efforts, but they aren't definitive answers. We still need to test and confirm whether these flagged areas are causing the bugs."

Collaborative Debugging: AI and Human Insight

With Codey's analysis as a guide, the team began working through each flagged section. They discovered that some of Codey's suggestions were directly related to the problem, while others needed additional investigation. Riley found that one of the logic flow gaps was indeed contributing to the bug, allowing certain edge cases to slip through unchecked.

"Codey got us halfway there," Riley commented, "but it missed the specific condition that was actually breaking the function. It's useful, but it still requires human follow-up."

Alex added, "Codey gives us direction, but we have to bring it to completion. It's saving us time on the initial search, but the final solution still depends on us."

Bob encouraged the team. "That's exactly the approach I want us to take. Codey is a tool for efficiency, but our expertise is still essential. It's the combination of AI and human insight that brings the best results."

Guidelines for AI-Assisted Debugging

After the debugging session, Bob gathered the team to outline best practices for using Codey in debugging. They discussed the balance between automation and expertise, and Bob presented guidelines for making the most of Codey's contributions:

- **Use AI as a Guide**: Let Codey identify potential problem areas, but verify each suggestion through testing and analysis.

- **Maintain Human Oversight**: AI can pinpoint patterns, but it's up to the team to determine whether those patterns indicate actual issues.

- **Document AI Contributions**: Keep a record of where AI suggestions were helpful and where further refinement was necessary, to guide future debugging sessions.

- **Combine AI and Manual Debugging**: Use Codey's insights to streamline initial exploration, then apply manual debugging techniques to finalize solutions.

- **Evaluate AI's Effectiveness**: Regularly assess how often AI suggestions lead to accurate resolutions, and refine the approach accordingly.

"We're building a process that's faster but still thorough," Bob said as they wrapped up the meeting. "With Codey handling the groundwork, we can focus on solving problems rather than just searching for them."

As the team left the meeting, each member felt a growing confidence in Codey's role in their workflow. Debugging, once a task of relentless trial and error, now had an element of strategy—and Codey was quickly becoming a valuable ally in the search for solutions.

Alex's Notebook

- Codey's debugging insights speed up the initial problem search.

- Important to remember that AI suggestions need human validation.

- Documenting AI-driven debugging helps refine future processes.

- Using Codey's guidance while trusting my own expertise is key.

- This process is efficient but requires critical thinking.

Jordan's Notebook

- Codey's suggestions give us a useful starting point in debugging.

- Learning to validate AI insights helps improve my problem-solving.

- Documenting AI contributions shows where it truly adds value.

- Excited to see how AI can continue streamlining our debugging process.

- Debugging feels more strategic with Codey as a partner.

Pat's Notebook

- Codey's ability to identify problem areas is a valuable time-saver.

- Human expertise is still essential for in-depth problem resolution.

- Documentation of AI suggestions enhances our debugging strategy.

- AI-driven insights need to be carefully vetted for accuracy.

- Optimistic about how AI can improve efficiency without sacrificing quality.

Riley's Notebook

- Codey's insights support faster debugging, but close validation is essential.

- Maintaining documentation of AI-suggested fixes aids in QA.

- AI can handle the routine checks, but our expertise ensures quality.

- Debugging feels more manageable with AI-driven direction.

- Cautiously optimistic about AI's role in QA for debugging.

Bob's Notebook

- AI-assisted debugging provides efficiency but requires careful validation.

- Documentation of AI-driven solutions is key to process refinement.

- Encouraging the team to balance AI efficiency with thorough testing.

- Confident that AI can support debugging when used thoughtfully.

- The team's expertise remains the core of our problem-solving.

Practical Advice

- Use AI tools to help locate potential issues in code quickly.

- Always review AI-driven insights to ensure accuracy and relevance.

- Track AI suggestions and document any adjustments made by the team.

- Balance AI-driven debugging with manual verification to ensure quality.

- Regularly assess AI's effectiveness in debugging to refine processes.

Implementation

- Begin by using AI to identify potential error zones and performance issues.

- Establish protocols for validating AI-driven debugging insights.

- Document outcomes of AI-assisted debugging for future reference.

- Use time saved by AI to focus on complex problem resolution.

- Continually review the balance between AI and manual debugging.

Real-World Insight

AI tools like DeepCode and CodeScene are increasingly used in debugging, where they analyze code to identify potential problem areas based on patterns and historical data. These tools enable developers to prioritize their debugging efforts more effectively, reducing time spent on preliminary analysis. However, the most effective use of AI in debugging combines automated insights with manual validation and problem-solving.

Pitfalls to Avoid

- Over-relying on AI for debugging without validating its suggestions.

- Failing to document AI-driven debugging efforts, missing critical insights.

- Allowing AI to overshadow the importance of manual problem-solving.

- Ignoring context-specific factors that require human expertise.

- Neglecting the need for balanced coverage between AI and manual debugging.

Self-Assessment

- How comfortable am I with using AI for debugging assistance?

- What areas of debugging can AI improve in my workflow?

- How can I ensure AI-driven insights align with our project requirements?

- What strategies can I use to validate AI suggestions effectively?

- How can AI support my role in maintaining high standards in problem-solving?

Self-Reflection

- Reflect on initial thoughts about AI in debugging—have they evolved?

- How do you see AI fitting into your debugging workflow going forward?

- Are there aspects of debugging where human oversight is crucial? Why?

- How can AI assist you in becoming a more efficient problem solver?

- What steps can you take to ensure a balanced approach with AI in debugging?

Chapter 6: AI in Code Review – First Impressions and Adjustments

Chapter 6: AI in Code Review – First Impressions and Adjustments

The team sat around the table as Bob prepared for today's meeting, projecting a complex codebase on the screen. Code reviews had always been a crucial part of their workflow, a practice that helped them maintain quality and spot potential issues early. Today, however, Bob wanted to introduce a new approach: using Codey to assist with initial code reviews.

"Alright, everyone," Bob began, "we're going to let Codey handle a first pass at code review today. The AI will highlight areas that might need attention, and then we'll go through to refine and review with our expertise."

Alex folded his arms, clearly skeptical. "Code review isn't just about finding errors—it's about understanding the purpose behind the code, making sure it aligns with the project goals. Can Codey really do that?"

"Not quite," Bob replied, acknowledging the concern. "Codey won't understand intent. But it can catch syntax errors, suggest optimizations, and flag potential security risks. Think of it as an initial filter that saves us time on the basics."

Riley looked intrigued. "If Codey can catch the small stuff, it might free us up to focus on the strategic parts of the review."

Bob nodded. "Exactly. Let's use it to clear away the routine checks so that we can dive deeper into the code's design and functionality."

Codey's First Code Review Pass

To give the team a firsthand look at Codey's capabilities in code review, Bob pulled up a recent module. He activated Codey's review function and watched as the AI quickly scanned through the code, highlighting several areas with recommendations:

- **Syntax Improvements**: Codey flagged a few syntax issues that could improve readability and performance.

- **Redundant Code Blocks**: It identified sections where redundant code could be consolidated or simplified.

- **Potential Security Vulnerabilities**: Codey flagged specific lines where security best practices weren't followed, suggesting alternative approaches.

Jordan leaned forward, impressed. "This would save us a lot of time! Normally, we'd spend a few passes just catching these kinds of issues."

Pat reviewed the flagged areas. "It's efficient, but it's not seeing the whole picture. Codey doesn't understand why certain lines are written a certain way. That's where we still come in."

Bob agreed. "That's the balance. Codey can get us part of the way, but a complete review will still rely on our judgment."

Balancing AI-Driven Review with Human Oversight

As the team worked through Codey's flagged areas, they began to see where AI could be most helpful—and where its limitations were apparent. For example, while Codey had caught potential security vulnerabilities, it didn't fully understand context, flagging some areas unnecessarily.

Riley pointed out, "Some of these flags are valid, but others are just conservative guesses. We'll need to validate each one to avoid unnecessary rewrites."

Bob nodded. "Exactly. Codey's suggestions are just that—suggestions. We're still the final decision-makers."

The team continued with the review, validating Codey's suggestions and adding their insights. Alex admitted, "I'm warming up to it. It's good for speeding up the initial checks, but we need to be careful not to lose the personal touch that makes our code high-quality."

Guidelines for AI-Assisted Code Review

After the code review session, Bob led a discussion on best practices for integrating AI into their review process, ensuring that Codey's efficiency complemented, rather than replaced, their expertise.

- **Use AI for Routine Checks**: Let Codey handle syntax, redundancy, and basic security scans, freeing up human resources for strategic analysis.

- **Maintain Human Oversight**: Validate all AI-flagged areas, as Codey cannot account for project-specific context.

- **Focus on High-Level Review**: Use AI for initial error detection, allowing team members to concentrate on code functionality, structure, and project alignment.

- **Document AI Contributions**: Track where Codey's insights were effective and where manual adjustments were needed.

- **Balance Efficiency with Depth**: Ensure that AI-driven reviews do not lead to shortcuts in areas that require detailed understanding.

"Codey can be a powerful tool in our review process," Bob concluded. "But we have to remember that a good code review is as much about understanding and intent as it is about catching errors. Let's use Codey to help us, but not to replace what makes our work unique."

The team left the meeting with a new perspective. Codey was proving to be a time-saver, but they were careful to maintain a balance between AI-driven insights and the deep understanding that only a human reviewer could bring.

Alex's Notebook

- Codey helps with routine code checks but can't replace in-depth reviews.

- Documenting AI suggestions shows where it adds value and where it misses.

- Balancing efficiency with careful review is key to maintaining quality.

- I'm seeing potential in AI-driven review, but we need to stay hands-on.

- Code review is still about understanding, not just error detection.

Jordan's Notebook

- Codey speeds up the basics, allowing us to focus on the bigger picture.

- Learning from AI's suggestions is helping refine my own code review skills.

- Documenting AI-driven changes shows its role in our workflow.

- Excited to see how AI can improve our code review process.

- Codey feels like a time-saver without compromising depth.

Pat's Notebook

- AI's syntax and security checks save time on routine parts of code review.

- Documenting AI-driven insights helps refine future code reviews.

- Balancing AI efficiency with human understanding ensures quality.

- AI-driven reviews complement our expertise but don't replace it.

- Codey's role in review is promising, but it requires careful oversight.

Riley's Notebook

- Codey supports efficiency in code review but needs close validation.
- Maintaining documentation of AI-driven suggestions ensures quality.
- AI handles routine tasks, allowing us to focus on strategic aspects.
- Code review still relies on human expertise to capture the full picture.
- Optimistic about using AI in code review, provided we maintain control.

Bob's Notebook

- AI-driven code review provides efficiency but requires validation.
- Documentation of AI suggestions is crucial for transparency and refinement.
- Encouraging the team to balance AI with manual code review efforts.
- Confident that AI can support code review when used thoughtfully.
- The team's expertise remains the foundation of our review quality.

Practical Advice

- Use AI tools to assist with routine syntax, security, and redundancy checks.
- Always validate AI suggestions to ensure alignment with project needs.
- Track AI-driven insights and document any manual adjustments for clarity.
- Balance AI-driven efficiency with manual code review for comprehensive quality.
- Focus human effort on high-level review aspects, such as structure and intent.

Implementation

- Begin by using AI for initial code review to catch syntax and security issues.

- Establish protocols for validating and documenting AI suggestions.

- Allocate saved time for deeper, strategic aspects of code review.

- Track outcomes of AI-driven reviews to guide future adjustments.

- Regularly assess the balance between AI and manual review to maintain quality.

Real-World Insight

In the software industry, companies increasingly use AI tools like SonarQube and Codacy to assist with code reviews. These tools handle routine checks efficiently, allowing developers to focus on higher-level analysis. However, successful code review workflows balance AI-driven efficiency with human oversight, ensuring that AI contributions complement the understanding that only a human reviewer can bring.

Pitfalls to Avoid

- Relying solely on AI for code review without manual validation.

- Failing to document AI-driven review efforts, leading to missed insights.

- Allowing AI efficiency to overshadow critical thinking in code review.

- Ignoring project-specific context in favor of AI-suggested changes.

- Neglecting the need for balanced review coverage between AI and manual input.

Self-Assessment

- How comfortable am I with using AI for code review assistance?

- What areas of code review can AI improve in my workflow?

- How can I ensure AI-driven reviews align with project goals?

- What strategies can I use to validate AI suggestions effectively?

- How can AI support my role in maintaining high standards in code review?

Self-Reflection

- Reflect on initial thoughts about AI in code review—have they evolved?

- How do you see AI fitting into your code review workflow moving forward?

- Are there aspects of code review where human oversight is crucial? Why?

- How can AI assist you in becoming a more efficient reviewer?

- What steps can you take to ensure a balanced approach with AI in code review?

Chapter 7: Pair Programming with AI – A New Kind of Partner

Chapter 7: Pair Programming with AI – A New Kind of Partner

The concept of pair programming was nothing new to the team. They often worked together on complex code, tackling challenges and bouncing ideas off one another. But today, Bob had something different in mind—pair programming with Codey.

"Alright, team," Bob began, addressing the group. "Today, I want you each to try a new type of collaboration. We're going to see how Codey can assist as a pair programming partner."

Jordan's eyes lit up with curiosity. "So, Codey is going to act like a second set of eyes?"

"Exactly," Bob replied. "Think of it as a coding partner who can suggest improvements, highlight potential errors, and help brainstorm solutions. But remember, it's still just a tool—it can't replace the problem-solving intuition that each of you brings."

Alex leaned back in his chair, skeptical but intrigued. "I'm open to trying it. But how useful can AI really be as a partner when it doesn't fully understand the purpose of the code?"

"That's the key," Bob responded. "Codey is here to support, not to take over. It's up to each of you to decide how you want to use its suggestions. Let's experiment and see where it adds value."

Pair Programming with Codey: First Impressions

To kick off the exercise, Bob assigned each team member a different task and asked them to pair up with Codey on their projects. Jordan, working on a new feature that required complex data manipulation, opened her code editor and activated Codey's assistance.

As she coded, Codey began to offer real-time suggestions:

- **Syntax Optimization**: Codey highlighted areas where Jordan could streamline her code for better readability.

- **Alternative Approaches**: For a particularly complex loop, Codey suggested a more efficient recursive function.

- **Error Prevention**: It flagged a variable that had not been initialized, preventing a potential runtime error.

Jordan was impressed by the AI's responsiveness. "It's like having a partner who's always alert to the little things," she noted, "and it's giving me ideas I wouldn't have thought of immediately."

Pat, on the other hand, was working on a complex algorithm. Codey's suggestions were helpful in catching minor errors and proposing optimizations, but Pat found that the AI struggled to fully grasp the algorithm's purpose.

"Codey is useful," Pat acknowledged, "but it doesn't understand the high-level logic. It's good at spotting surface issues, but the deeper insights still need a human touch."

The Balance of Control and Collaboration

As each team member experimented with Codey's pair programming features, they quickly learned that the partnership required balance. While Codey could accelerate the coding process by handling minor adjustments and catching errors, its suggestions sometimes conflicted with their planned approach or missed the broader context.

Riley found Codey's assistance particularly useful in identifying edge cases for her test scripts. "It's great at pointing out areas where bugs might slip through," she said, "but I still have to decide which cases are relevant to our project. It's like working with a junior developer who's eager to help but still learning the ropes."

Alex, who had initially been doubtful, admitted that Codey's speed and consistency were impressive. "It's like having a partner who's always on top of the details, but I have to stay in control. Codey's suggestions are helpful, but it's still up to me to decide if they make sense."

Guidelines for Pair Programming with AI

After the session, Bob gathered the team to discuss their experiences and establish guidelines for effectively using Codey as a pair programming assistant.

- **Use AI for Routine Assistance**: Let Codey handle minor syntax adjustments, error prevention, and alternative code suggestions to save time on routine aspects.

- **Maintain Control**: Treat Codey's suggestions as advisory, making final decisions based on project goals and context.

- **Document AI Interactions**: Track when Codey's suggestions were accepted or modified to help refine future interactions.

- **Balance Automation with Human Intuition**: Rely on Codey for efficiency but apply personal expertise to ensure code quality.

- **Encourage Experimentation**: Use Codey's suggestions to explore new ideas, but validate them against your understanding.

"Codey can be a valuable partner," Bob concluded, "but remember, it's still learning from us. We're in charge, and our expertise shapes its role. Let's use this to our advantage while maintaining control over our code."

The team left with a renewed perspective. Codey was more than just a tool; it was a new kind of coding partner—one that could suggest, support, and even challenge, but always required human oversight to bring projects to life.

Alex's Notebook

- Codey's real-time suggestions speed up coding, but human oversight is essential.

- Documenting AI-driven changes helps track where it's effective.

- Maintaining control is key; AI suggestions need context to be valuable.

- I'm seeing potential in AI-driven pair programming, but we need to stay hands-on.

- It's a helpful partner, but only with careful oversight.

Jordan's Notebook

- Codey's real-time suggestions are like having an always-alert partner.

- AI's suggestions help refine my own coding approach.

- Documenting AI contributions shows where it adds value to our work.

- Excited about how AI can improve our workflow.

- Codey feels like a supportive partner for the details.

Pat's Notebook

- Codey's suggestions are helpful for routine checks but lack deeper insight.

- Balancing AI efficiency with human expertise ensures quality.

- Documenting AI-driven changes enhances our understanding of its role.

- AI assists with coding details but doesn't replace intuition.

- Optimistic about how AI can improve efficiency without losing depth.

Riley's Notebook

- Codey's assistance is helpful for catching edge cases but needs validation.

- Maintaining documentation of AI-driven changes aids in QA.

- AI can handle routine suggestions, freeing us to focus on strategic work.

- Pair programming with AI still relies on human expertise for full context.

- Cautiously optimistic about AI's role in pair programming.

Bob's Notebook

- AI-driven pair programming provides efficiency but requires control.

- Documentation of AI suggestions is crucial for transparency and refinement.

- Encouraging the team to balance AI with manual coding efforts.

- Confident that AI can support pair programming when used thoughtfully.

- The team's expertise remains the foundation of our programming quality.

Practical Advice

- Use AI tools to assist with routine pair programming tasks, such as syntax and error checking.

- Always validate AI-driven suggestions to ensure they align with project goals.

- Track AI-driven insights and document any modifications made by the team.

- Balance AI-driven efficiency with manual coding for comprehensive quality.

- Treat AI as a supportive partner, relying on human expertise to guide its role.

Implementation

- Start by using AI for routine checks and basic suggestions in pair programming.

- Establish protocols for validating and documenting AI-driven contributions.

- Use time saved by AI to focus on complex, high-value coding tasks.

- Regularly assess the balance between AI and manual coding efforts.

- Encourage experimentation to see where AI-driven pair programming adds value.

Real-World Insight

In modern software development, pair programming with AI is gaining traction as a way to streamline coding tasks and reduce errors. Tools like GitHub Copilot and Tabnine offer real-time suggestions, assisting developers with syntax, structure, and bug prevention. However, the most effective implementations balance AI's support with human control, allowing AI to enhance efficiency without compromising coding quality.

Pitfalls to Avoid

- Relying solely on AI for pair programming without validating suggestions.

- Failing to document AI-driven changes, leading to missed insights.

- Allowing AI efficiency to overshadow critical thinking in coding.

- Ignoring project-specific context in favor of AI suggestions.

- Neglecting the need for balanced collaboration between AI and human input.

Self-Assessment

- How comfortable am I with using AI for pair programming assistance?

- What areas of pair programming can AI improve in my workflow?

- How can I ensure AI-driven suggestions align with project goals?

- What strategies can I use to validate AI suggestions effectively?

- How can AI support my role in maintaining high standards in coding?

Self-Reflection

- Reflect on initial thoughts about AI in pair programming—have they evolved?

- How do you see AI fitting into your pair programming workflow going forward?

- Are there aspects of pair programming where human oversight is crucial? Why?

- How can AI assist you in becoming a more efficient coder?

- What steps can you take to ensure a balanced approach with AI in pair programming?

Chapter 8: AI-Driven Refactoring – Efficiency or Risk?

Chapter 8: AI-Driven Refactoring – Efficiency or Risk?

Refactoring was a task the team had grown to respect and occasionally dread. While it was essential to keep their codebase clean and optimized, it often felt like they were unraveling a tightly wound knot. Today, Bob wanted to see how Codey could contribute to this process.

"Alright, team," Bob began, addressing the group. "Today, we're going to try something different. Codey will assist us with refactoring. The goal is to see if it can help us spot areas for optimization and improve efficiency without sacrificing the integrity of our code."

Pat, the team's architect, leaned forward with interest. "Refactoring is complex—it's not just about cutting down code but ensuring it stays maintainable and robust. Can Codey handle that level of detail?"

"Good question," Bob replied. "Codey will provide suggestions for simplification and efficiency, but we'll need to validate each change. This is where our expertise comes in. We're not giving Codey free rein; we're using it as a guide."

Jordan looked excited. "So, it'll be like a partner suggesting improvements, but we still make the final call?"

"Exactly," Bob affirmed. "Think of it as a second opinion that can save us time on routine refactoring, while we focus on the strategic aspects."

Codey's First Pass at Refactoring

Bob selected a module with known inefficiencies, giving Codey access to analyze it for possible improvements. Within moments, Codey flagged several areas with recommendations:

- **Code Simplification**: Codey suggested consolidating repetitive blocks and reducing nested conditionals for clarity.

- **Memory Optimization**: It flagged instances where memory could be conserved by reusing objects rather than creating new ones.

- **Function Extraction**: Codey proposed breaking down a complex function into smaller, reusable functions to improve readability and reduce duplication.

Riley examined Codey's suggestions, nodding thoughtfully. "These are good suggestions, but we'll need to check if breaking down functions impacts other modules. We don't want to introduce issues with dependencies."

Chapter 8: AI-Driven Refactoring – Efficiency or Risk?

Alex, who was more skeptical, reviewed the proposed memory optimizations. "Codey's suggestions are solid, but they're generic. It's pointing out potential improvements without fully understanding our code's purpose."

"That's why we're here," Bob said. "Codey gives us a starting point, but we validate each change and consider the bigger picture. Let's see where these suggestions take us."

Balancing AI Suggestions with Practical Constraints

As the team applied Codey's refactoring suggestions, they quickly saw the benefits in some areas and the limitations in others. For instance, Codey's recommendations for simplifying nested conditions improved readability and even slightly boosted performance. However, its more aggressive suggestions, like extracting functions, sometimes required careful consideration to avoid disrupting the flow of the code.

Pat noted, "Codey's suggestions for smaller functions are helpful, but we need to make sure they don't complicate things down the line. Sometimes simpler isn't always better."

Jordan found Codey's simplification recommendations helpful, particularly in consolidating repetitive code. "It's like having a fresh set of eyes that spots the obvious patterns we overlook."

Bob encouraged the team. "This is where the balance comes in. Codey can help us cut down on routine tasks, but we're responsible for ensuring the code remains reliable and maintainable."

Guidelines for AI-Assisted Refactoring

After the refactoring session, Bob gathered the team to establish guidelines for effectively using Codey in refactoring. These principles would help the team maximize AI-driven suggestions while maintaining control over code quality.

- **Use AI for Routine Optimization**: Allow Codey to suggest improvements for repetitive and routine code patterns to streamline the process.

- **Maintain Contextual Awareness**: Validate each suggestion in the context of the project's specific requirements, ensuring changes don't impact functionality.

- **Document AI Contributions**: Keep a record of AI-driven refactoring efforts to support debugging and future maintenance.

- **Balance Simplicity and Complexity**: Use Codey to simplify where it adds value, but avoid excessive function extraction if it adds complexity.

- **Encourage Incremental Changes**: Apply AI-driven refactoring in stages, testing each change for impact before moving to the next.

"Refactoring with AI is about finding efficiencies without sacrificing quality," Bob concluded. "Codey can make our lives easier, but only if we guide it carefully. Let's keep this balance as we move forward."

The team left with a new respect for AI in refactoring. Codey was proving to be a powerful ally, helping them cut through routine work while allowing them to focus on what truly mattered: clean, maintainable code that aligned with their project goals.

Alex's Notebook

- Codey's suggestions streamline routine refactoring, but oversight is crucial.

- Documenting AI-driven changes helps with future debugging.

- Balancing simplicity and functionality is key in refactoring.

- AI-driven improvements are helpful but need context-specific validation.

- Refactoring with AI is efficient, but we need to control the process.

Jordan's Notebook

- Codey's refactoring suggestions save time on repetitive tasks.

- Documenting AI contributions shows where it adds value to our work.

- Balancing efficiency and complexity ensures code remains maintainable.

- AI-driven simplifications improve readability without compromising depth.

- Excited to see how AI continues to streamline our workflow.

Pat's Notebook

- AI-driven refactoring can improve efficiency, but validation is essential.
- Maintaining control ensures Codey's suggestions don't disrupt functionality.
- Documenting AI-driven changes supports long-term code quality.
- Codey assists in routine tasks but requires careful oversight.
- Optimistic about AI's role in simplifying complex refactoring.

Riley's Notebook

- Codey's suggestions help streamline refactoring but need validation.
- Maintaining documentation of AI-driven changes aids in QA.
- AI handles routine improvements, allowing us to focus on core functionality.
- Refactoring still relies on expertise to balance simplicity and usability.
- Cautiously optimistic about AI's role in code improvement.

Bob's Notebook

- AI-driven refactoring provides efficiency but requires careful validation.
- Documentation of AI contributions is crucial for transparency and quality.
- Encouraging the team to balance AI with manual refactoring efforts.
- Confident that AI can support refactoring when used thoughtfully.
- The team's expertise remains the foundation of our code quality.

Practical Advice

- Use AI tools to suggest routine refactoring improvements, such as simplification and optimization.

- Always validate AI-driven refactoring suggestions to ensure alignment with project goals.

- Track AI-driven insights and document any modifications made by the team.

- Balance AI-driven simplification with maintainability, avoiding excessive changes.

- Treat AI as a support tool in refactoring, using human expertise to guide its role.

Implementation

- Start by using AI for routine optimization and simplification suggestions in refactoring.

- Establish protocols for validating and documenting AI-driven contributions.

- Apply AI suggestions incrementally, testing each change for stability and impact.

- Regularly assess the balance between AI-driven and manual refactoring to maintain quality.

- Encourage experimentation to find where AI-driven refactoring adds the most value.

Real-World Insight

AI tools are increasingly used in code refactoring to improve readability, performance, and maintainability. Companies employ tools like Refactoring.Guru and SonarQube to streamline refactoring tasks, allowing developers to focus on higher-level code quality. While AI-driven refactoring saves time, the most effective results combine AI insights with human oversight to ensure code remains maintainable and aligned with project goals.

Pitfalls to Avoid

- Over-relying on AI for refactoring without validating suggestions.

- Failing to document AI-driven changes, leading to maintenance issues.

- Allowing AI efficiency to overshadow the need for maintainable code.

- Ignoring project-specific context in favor of AI-suggested changes.

- Neglecting the need for balanced refactoring between AI and manual input.

Self-Assessment

- How comfortable am I with using AI for refactoring assistance?

- What areas of refactoring can AI improve in my workflow?

- How can I ensure AI-driven refactoring aligns with project requirements?

- What strategies can I use to validate AI suggestions effectively?

- How can AI support my role in maintaining high standards in code quality?

Self-Reflection

- Reflect on initial thoughts about AI in refactoring—have they evolved?

- How do you see AI fitting into your refactoring workflow going forward?

- Are there aspects of refactoring where human oversight is crucial? Why?

- How can AI assist you in becoming more efficient in code improvement?

- What steps can you take to ensure a balanced approach with AI in refactoring?

Chapter 9: AI in Security – Shield or Blind Spot?

Chapter 9: AI in Security – Shield or Blind Spot?

Security was a critical pillar of every project the team worked on. While they had strong protocols in place, they knew that even small vulnerabilities could lead to significant issues. Today, Bob wanted to see if Codey could play a role in their security practices, identifying weak points that might otherwise be overlooked.

"Today, we're going to test Codey's ability to enhance our security reviews," Bob began, addressing the team. "Security is non-negotiable for us, and if Codey can help us spot potential vulnerabilities faster, it could make a real difference in our process."

Riley, who managed much of the team's security testing, looked intrigued. "So, Codey will be scanning for common vulnerabilities?"

"Exactly," Bob replied. "Codey can analyze code for typical security risks—unsecured data handling, risky variable declarations, and access control issues. However, Codey won't catch everything, and it doesn't fully understand the context, so we still need to validate each finding."

Pat nodded, echoing the sentiment. "Security is one of those areas where a single oversight can create a huge vulnerability. AI can be a big help, but we have to make sure we're not relying on it blindly."

"Precisely," Bob affirmed. "Think of Codey as an extra layer of defense. Let's see where it's helpful, but we'll still need our expertise to make sure nothing slips through."

Codey's First Security Scan

To give Codey a test run, Bob selected a recent module and instructed Codey to scan for potential security vulnerabilities. Within moments, Codey flagged several areas with recommendations:

- **Data Handling Risks**: Codey flagged instances where sensitive data was stored without encryption, suggesting encryption methods to mitigate risk.

- **Input Validation**: It highlighted places where user inputs weren't fully validated, which could lead to injection attacks or unexpected behavior.

- **Access Control**: Codey identified a function that allowed broader access than intended, recommending adjustments to restrict user permissions.

Jordan reviewed the flagged areas, nodding thoughtfully. "These are good catches. Normally, it would take us several passes to identify these types of issues."

Chapter 9: AI in Security – Shield or Blind Spot?

Riley, however, noticed that some of Codey's warnings were overly cautious. "It's flagging places where our data is already encrypted. Codey doesn't seem to recognize our existing protocols."

"That's where we come in," Bob said. "Codey can help us catch the basics, but we still need to make sure its suggestions align with our practices. Let's go through each flagged area and validate its relevance."

Balancing AI-Driven Security with Human Oversight

As the team reviewed Codey's suggestions, they quickly realized that while the AI's insights were valuable, they required contextual interpretation. Codey's data handling flags, for instance, identified potential security risks that had already been mitigated by existing protocols. On the other hand, its recommendations for input validation highlighted areas the team had missed, prompting them to make necessary updates.

Alex, who was initially skeptical, admitted, "Codey's suggestions are thorough, but it's a bit overzealous. It catches the obvious vulnerabilities, but we need to sift through them to see what actually matters."

Bob nodded. "Exactly. Codey's a useful tool for getting a head start, but we're still the ones who make the call on what's relevant. Let's use it as a guide rather than a replacement."

The team continued validating Codey's recommendations, applying changes where needed and dismissing redundant warnings. Riley appreciated how Codey streamlined the initial review but remained cautious about trusting its suggestions without oversight. "It's a great help, but we're still responsible for making sure every area is fully secure."

Guidelines for AI-Assisted Security

After the security review session, Bob led a discussion to establish best practices for using Codey in their security processes, ensuring a balanced approach between AI insights and human expertise.

- **Use AI for Initial Security Scans**: Let Codey handle basic scans for common security risks, such as input validation and access control.

- **Maintain Rigorous Validation**: Review and validate each AI-flagged area, ensuring suggestions align with the team's security protocols.

- **Document AI-Driven Security Changes**: Track where AI suggestions led to actual changes and where redundant warnings were dismissed.

- **Combine AI and Manual Checks**: Use Codey to handle the initial pass, then conduct a thorough manual review to ensure no context-specific risks are overlooked.

- **Encourage Continuous Improvement**: Regularly assess Codey's security scans to refine its role in the security process.

"AI can be an effective shield," Bob concluded, "but it's only one layer of our defense. Codey gives us a head start, but we still need to bring our judgment and knowledge to ensure full security coverage."

The team left with a renewed appreciation for Codey's role in enhancing their security workflow. While AI was proving to be a valuable asset, they knew that human vigilance remained essential to maintaining a secure, robust codebase.

Alex's Notebook

- Codey helps with initial security scans but needs validation.

- Documenting AI-driven security changes keeps track of its effectiveness.

- Balancing AI with manual checks ensures thorough coverage.

- AI-driven security review is helpful but requires critical oversight.

- Security still relies on human vigilance for context and depth.

Jordan's Notebook

- Codey's suggestions streamline the initial security review.

- Learning to validate AI insights improves my understanding of security.

- Documenting AI-driven changes shows its impact on our process.

- Excited about how AI can support our security efforts.

- Codey feels like a useful layer in our security defense.

Pat's Notebook

- AI-driven security checks provide a valuable head start.

- Maintaining control ensures Codey's suggestions don't conflict with protocols.

- Documenting AI contributions supports continuous improvement in security.

- AI assists in routine security tasks but requires careful oversight.

- Optimistic about AI's role in improving efficiency without losing depth.

Riley's Notebook

- Codey's security insights are helpful but need close validation.

- Maintaining documentation of AI-driven security changes aids in QA.

- AI handles routine risks, allowing us to focus on complex threats.

- Security still relies on expertise to understand full context.

- Cautiously optimistic about AI's role in security review.

Bob's Notebook

- AI-driven security provides efficiency but requires rigorous validation.

- Documentation of AI contributions is crucial for transparency and improvement.

- Encouraging the team to balance AI with manual security efforts.

- Confident that AI can support security when used thoughtfully.

- The team's expertise remains the foundation of our security quality.

Practical Advice

- Use AI tools to assist with routine security scans, such as data handling and access control checks.

- Always validate AI-driven security suggestions to ensure they align with project requirements.

- Track AI-driven security insights and document any modifications for clarity.

- Balance AI-driven security with manual checks for comprehensive coverage.

- Treat AI as a supportive layer in security, relying on human oversight to guide its role.

Implementation

- Start by using AI for initial security scans to catch common vulnerabilities.

- Establish protocols for validating and documenting AI-driven security changes.

- Use AI-driven insights as a guide, but apply manual checks for thoroughness.

- Regularly assess the balance between AI and manual security checks to maintain quality.

- Encourage continuous improvement to refine AI's role in the security process.

Real-World Insight

Many companies employ AI tools to assist with security, using platforms like Checkmarx and Veracode to identify vulnerabilities and automate initial scans. While AI-driven security review is efficient, the best practices combine automated insights with human oversight, ensuring comprehensive security coverage that addresses both common risks and context-specific concerns.

Pitfalls to Avoid

- Relying solely on AI for security without validating suggestions.

- Failing to document AI-driven security changes, leading to missed insights.

- Allowing AI efficiency to overshadow the need for comprehensive security.

- Ignoring project-specific security requirements in favor of AI suggestions.

- Neglecting the need for balanced coverage between AI and manual security checks.

Self-Assessment

- How comfortable am I with using AI for security assistance?

- What areas of security can AI improve in my workflow?

- How can I ensure AI-driven security checks align with project requirements?

- What strategies can I use to validate AI suggestions effectively?

- How can AI support my role in maintaining high standards in security?

Self-Reflection

- Reflect on initial thoughts about AI in security—have they evolved?

- How do you see AI fitting into your security workflow moving forward?

- Are there aspects of security where human oversight is crucial? Why?

- How can AI assist you in becoming more effective in security?

- What steps can you take to ensure a balanced approach with AI in security?

Chapter 10: AI in Deployment – Streamlining or Complicating Processes?

Chapter 10: AI in Deployment – Streamlining or Complicating Processes?

Deployment days were always high-stakes for the team. With their code finalized, it was crucial that everything went smoothly from development to production. The pressure was on, and Bob wanted to see if Codey could assist in streamlining their deployment process, catching potential issues before they reached production.

"Today, we're going to test how Codey can help us with deployment," Bob announced to the team. "The goal is to ensure our deployment is smooth and as error-free as possible. Codey will help us review our deployment scripts, configurations, and dependencies to catch potential issues early."

Jordan, excited but cautious, raised a hand. "Deployment can be unpredictable. Can Codey really help us anticipate the unknowns?"

"That's what we're here to find out," Bob replied. "Codey won't catch everything, but it can help us by running through checks and suggesting optimizations. We'll be able to go into deployment with a stronger level of confidence."

Just as the team was gearing up, the conference room door opened. Zoey stepped in, a familiar smile on her face. "I heard you were bringing AI into deployment and thought I'd drop by to share some of my own experiences."

The team was thrilled to see Zoey, knowing her expertise with AI in project management. Bob introduced her to Codey and explained their goals for using AI in deployment.

Zoey's Encouragement and Advice

Zoey smiled, remembering her own journey. "I know firsthand how AI can transform workflows and help catch issues we might miss. The key is to trust its insights but still bring our own expertise into the process. AI is here to support, not replace, what we know."

Pat looked curious. "Did you find that AI really improved your deployment processes?"

Zoey nodded. "Absolutely. The AI I used helped identify misconfigurations and even pinpointed a few potential bottlenecks that we might have missed. But the real value came from combining its recommendations with our understanding of the project's goals and requirements. It saved us time, but it also gave us new perspectives on efficiency."

Alex, still a bit skeptical, asked, "So, how do we balance relying on AI with making sure we don't lose control of the process?"

Chapter 10: AI in Deployment – Streamlining or Complicating Processes?

"Great question," Zoey replied. "It's all about control and collaboration. AI can handle the repetitive, routine checks that can be easy to overlook in a rush. But you're still the experts. Use it as an extra layer of review—don't see it as a replacement. You'll find that it frees you up to focus on what matters most."

Codey's Role in Deployment

Inspired by Zoey's advice, the team set up Codey to assist with their deployment checks. Bob selected a module ready for deployment and activated Codey to scan the deployment scripts, configurations, and dependencies.

Within moments, Codey highlighted a few areas with potential issues:

- **Configuration Mismatches**: Codey flagged a configuration file that didn't align with the production environment settings, suggesting updates to avoid potential errors.

- **Dependency Conflicts**: It identified two libraries with conflicting versions that could cause issues if not updated before deployment.

- **Performance Bottlenecks**: Codey noted that certain database queries in the deployment pipeline could be optimized to reduce load times.

Jordan was impressed. "These are issues that might have taken us a while to catch on our own. Codey's speeding up our review."

Riley examined the flagged areas. "But we still need to validate each suggestion. Deployment is high-stakes—one overlooked issue could have a major impact."

Bob agreed. "Exactly. Codey gives us a head start, but we're still responsible for every part of the deployment process. Let's take each suggestion and make sure it aligns with our production needs."

Balancing AI in Deployment with Human Oversight

Following Zoey's advice, the team took a balanced approach, reviewing each of Codey's suggestions. They found that some flagged areas were indeed potential risks that needed attention, while others required context-specific adjustments.

Pat found that Codey's configuration warnings were valid, helping them catch mismatches that would have disrupted the deployment. However, some dependency conflicts needed to be addressed with careful consideration of the project's requirements, which Codey couldn't fully grasp.

Zoey observed their process, nodding approvingly. "You're doing it right—letting AI handle the routine checks while you focus on the bigger picture."

Before she left, Zoey offered one last piece of advice. "Embrace the efficiency that AI brings, but don't be afraid to question it. You're the experts, and your insight makes the difference between a successful deployment and a near-miss."

The team thanked her, feeling motivated and more confident in their approach with Codey. Zoey's encouragement had helped them see AI not as a replacement but as a collaborative tool, empowering them to refine their deployment process.

Guidelines for AI-Assisted Deployment

After Zoey's visit, Bob gathered the team to outline best practices for using Codey in their deployment process, ensuring a careful balance between AI insights and human expertise.

- **Use AI for Routine Checks**: Allow Codey to handle configuration alignment, dependency checks, and performance scans, giving the team time to focus on critical areas.

- **Maintain Final Oversight**: Review and validate each AI-suggested change, ensuring that all adjustments meet production requirements.

- **Document AI Contributions**: Track which AI-driven suggestions were implemented and where modifications were necessary, providing a record for future deployments.

- **Combine AI and Manual Review**: Use Codey for the initial pass, then conduct a thorough manual review to ensure full readiness.

- **Embrace Continuous Improvement**: Regularly assess the deployment process, refining Codey's role to maximize efficiency without sacrificing control.

"We've got a great tool in Codey," Bob concluded, "but let's remember that our expertise is what ensures a successful deployment. AI gives us efficiency, but it's our knowledge that ensures quality."

The team left with a renewed commitment to their deployment process, feeling encouraged by Zoey's visit and empowered by Codey's support. They knew that with AI as a partner, they could streamline their workflow without compromising their standards.

Alex's Notebook

- Codey's suggestions streamline deployment, but validation is key.
- Documenting AI-driven deployment changes helps track its impact.
- Balancing AI with manual review is crucial for a smooth deployment.
- AI adds value, but we're still responsible for final quality.
- Deployment feels more manageable with AI support.

Jordan's Notebook

- Codey's checks speed up deployment, catching potential issues early.
- Learning to validate AI insights refines my understanding of deployment.
- Documenting AI-driven changes supports continuous improvement.
- AI makes deployment feel less daunting with its proactive checks.
- Excited to see how AI can streamline future deployments.

Pat's Notebook

- AI-driven checks catch deployment issues but require oversight.
- Maintaining control ensures Codey's suggestions align with our requirements.
- Documenting AI contributions helps refine our deployment process.
- AI assists with routine checks but requires careful validation.
- Optimistic about AI's role in efficient, safe deployments.

Riley's Notebook

- Codey's deployment checks are helpful but need validation.
- Maintaining documentation of AI-driven changes aids in quality assurance.

- AI can handle routine issues, letting us focus on critical checks.

- Deployment is smoother with AI as a support, but we still need oversight.

- Cautiously optimistic about AI's role in deployment.

Bob's Notebook

- AI-driven deployment improves efficiency but requires validation.

- Documentation of AI contributions is key to transparency and quality.

- Encouraging the team to balance AI with manual deployment efforts.

- Confident that AI can support deployment when used thoughtfully.

- The team's expertise remains the foundation of our deployment quality.

Practical Advice

- Use AI tools to assist with routine deployment checks, such as configuration and dependency reviews.

- Always validate AI-driven deployment suggestions to ensure they meet production standards.

- Track AI-driven insights and document any modifications for future improvement.

- Balance AI-driven efficiency with manual review for comprehensive deployment quality.

- Treat AI as a support tool in deployment, relying on human oversight to guide its role.

Implementation

- Start by using AI for initial deployment checks to catch common issues.

- Establish protocols for validating and documenting AI-driven deployment changes.

- Use AI-driven insights as a foundation, then apply manual checks for readiness.

- Regularly assess the balance between AI and manual deployment review to maintain quality.

- Encourage continuous improvement to refine AI's role in the deployment process.

Real-World Insight

In the software industry, companies increasingly use AI tools like Harness and Octopus Deploy to assist with deployment, streamlining processes and automating checks. AI-driven deployment tools catch configuration and dependency issues early, reducing the risk of production errors. However, effective deployment requires combining AI efficiency with human oversight to ensure full quality and alignment with production requirements.

Pitfalls to Avoid

- Relying solely on AI for deployment checks without manual validation.

- Failing to document AI-driven deployment changes, leading to missed insights.

- Allowing AI efficiency to overshadow the need for thorough deployment review.

- Ignoring project-specific requirements in favor of AI suggestions.

- Neglecting the need for balanced review between AI and manual deployment checks.

Self-Assessment

- How comfortable am I with using AI for deployment assistance?

- What areas of deployment can AI improve in my workflow?

- How can I ensure AI-driven deployment checks align with project requirements?

- What strategies can I use to validate AI suggestions effectively?
- How can AI support my role in maintaining high standards in deployment?

Self-Reflection

- Reflect on initial thoughts about AI in deployment—have they evolved?
- How do you see AI fitting into your deployment workflow going forward?
- Are there aspects of deployment where human oversight is crucial? Why?
- How can AI assist you in becoming more efficient in deployment?
- What steps can you take to ensure a balanced approach with AI in deployment?

Chapter 11: AI in Optimization – Magic Bullet or Just Another Tool?

Chapter 11: AI in Optimization – Magic Bullet or Just Another Tool?

The team knew that optimization could make or break their projects. Efficient code meant faster load times, better performance, and fewer resource demands—benefits that were crucial, especially as their applications scaled. Today, Bob wanted to see how Codey could contribute to this essential process.

"Alright, team," Bob began, addressing the group. "We're going to try something new today: using Codey to help us with code optimization. The idea is to let Codey identify areas where our code can be streamlined for better performance."

Riley, who handled a lot of performance testing, looked intrigued. "So, Codey's going to analyze for inefficiencies and suggest changes?"

"Exactly," Bob replied. "Codey can highlight areas where we might improve memory usage, reduce execution time, or streamline processing. However, it's up to us to validate each suggestion to make sure it fits with our project's requirements and constraints."

Alex, ever the skeptic, raised a brow. "Optimization is more than just cutting down code. Codey might make suggestions that improve speed but compromise functionality."

"Good point," Bob agreed. "Our job is to balance Codey's efficiency suggestions with practicality. Let's see where it can add value, but we'll be the ones deciding if each change makes sense."

Codey's Optimization Suggestions

To give Codey a test run, Bob selected a module with known performance bottlenecks and asked Codey to analyze it for potential optimizations. Within moments, Codey displayed its first round of suggestions:

- **Memory Optimization**: Codey recommended reusing objects instead of creating new instances to save memory.

- **Loop Efficiency**: It suggested restructuring certain loops to reduce processing time, highlighting a nested loop as a prime candidate for optimization.

- **Query Optimization**: Codey identified a database query that could be streamlined, potentially speeding up data retrieval.

Pat examined Codey's suggestions closely. "These look like sound recommendations, but we need to check if reusing objects might introduce unintended side effects."

Chapter 11: AI in Optimization – Magic Bullet or Just Another Tool?

Jordan, reviewing the database optimization, nodded. "This query improvement could be useful, but we'll need to test it thoroughly to make sure it doesn't break anything downstream."

Bob encouraged the team. "This is exactly the approach I want us to take. Codey is here to offer ideas, but we're the ones responsible for making sure they fit with our overall project goals."

Balancing AI-Driven Optimization with Practicality

As the team worked through Codey's recommendations, they discovered that while some of the suggestions were beneficial, others required careful consideration. Codey's memory optimization was helpful in reducing resource use, but they realized it was more applicable in isolated parts of the code. For complex sections that handled user data, the AI-driven changes needed close review to ensure they wouldn't introduce new issues.

Riley found Codey's loop efficiency suggestions particularly useful. "This change will definitely save processing time. It's a small tweak, but it could make a big difference at scale."

However, Alex raised a cautionary note. "Codey's recommendations need to be tested rigorously. Optimization can improve performance, but if it comes at the cost of maintainability or functionality, we're going to have problems down the line."

Bob agreed. "Optimization is about balance. Codey can give us a head start, but we're still responsible for ensuring each change aligns with the project's needs and constraints."

Guidelines for AI-Assisted Optimization

After the optimization session, Bob gathered the team to outline best practices for using Codey in their optimization process. These guidelines would help them maximize AI-driven suggestions without sacrificing quality or maintainability.

- **Use AI for Routine Optimizations**: Allow Codey to handle repetitive tasks like loop restructuring and memory suggestions, streamlining basic performance improvements.

- **Validate AI Recommendations**: Review each AI suggestion, testing it to confirm that it enhances performance without compromising functionality.

- **Document AI-Driven Changes**: Track where AI recommendations were implemented and where modifications were necessary for clarity and future debugging.

- **Balance Efficiency with Practicality**: Use AI to save time, but prioritize maintainability and usability, ensuring changes are sustainable.

- **Encourage Incremental Optimization**: Apply AI-driven optimizations in stages, testing each improvement before implementing it across the project.

"Codey can be a great tool in our optimization efforts," Bob concluded. "But remember, optimization is as much an art as it is a science. AI gives us efficiency, but it's our expertise that ensures every change is practical."

The team left with a clear understanding of how to balance AI-driven optimization with their judgment. They felt encouraged by Codey's contributions and empowered to make smarter, faster decisions that would benefit the performance of their applications.

Alex's Notebook

- Codey's suggestions streamline basic optimization, but oversight is essential.

- Documenting AI-driven changes keeps track of effectiveness and impact.

- Balancing AI recommendations with functionality is key to sustainable optimization.

- Optimization with AI is efficient but requires careful validation.

- Optimization is more than performance; it's about maintainability too.

Jordan's Notebook

- Codey's suggestions help streamline repetitive tasks, saving time.

- Learning from AI's approach refines my understanding of optimization.

- Documenting AI contributions shows its impact on our workflow.

- Excited to see how AI can continue to improve our performance.
- Codey feels like a useful partner in our optimization efforts.

Pat's Notebook

- AI-driven optimization saves time but needs context-specific validation.
- Documenting changes is crucial to maintain code clarity and quality.
- Balance between AI-driven efficiency and practical needs is essential.
- Optimistic about how AI can improve efficiency without sacrificing quality.
- Codey's role in optimization is helpful, but human insight is critical.

Riley's Notebook

- Codey's optimization suggestions are helpful but need validation.
- Maintaining documentation of AI-driven changes aids in quality assurance.
- AI handles routine improvements, letting us focus on complex performance.
- Optimization is smoother with AI as a support, but we still need oversight.
- Cautiously optimistic about AI's role in improving efficiency.

Bob's Notebook

- AI-driven optimization provides efficiency but requires critical oversight.
- Documentation of AI contributions is key to transparency and improvement.
- Encouraging the team to balance AI with manual optimization efforts.
- Confident that AI can support optimization when used thoughtfully.
- The team's expertise remains the foundation of our code quality.

Practical Advice

- Use AI tools to assist with routine optimizations, such as loop and memory adjustments.

- Always validate AI-driven optimization suggestions to ensure alignment with project goals.

- Track AI-driven insights and document any modifications for clarity and future reference.

- Balance AI-driven efficiency with practical considerations for comprehensive code quality.

- Treat AI as a support tool in optimization, using human expertise to guide its role.

Implementation

- Start by using AI for initial optimization checks to catch common inefficiencies.

- Establish protocols for validating and documenting AI-driven optimization changes.

- Apply AI-driven suggestions incrementally, testing each change for impact.

- Regularly assess the balance between AI and manual optimization efforts.

- Encourage continuous improvement to refine AI's role in the optimization process.

Real-World Insight

AI-driven optimization tools, such as Dynatrace and AppDynamics, help software teams identify performance bottlenecks and improve efficiency. These tools allow developers to streamline tasks, reducing load times and memory usage. However, successful optimization combines AI's insights with human validation, ensuring performance improvements align with usability, maintainability, and project goals.

Pitfalls to Avoid

- Relying solely on AI for optimization without validating suggestions.

- Failing to document AI-driven optimization changes, leading to maintenance issues.

- Allowing AI efficiency to overshadow the need for maintainable code.

- Ignoring project-specific requirements in favor of AI suggestions.

- Neglecting the need for balanced optimization between AI and manual input.

Self-Assessment

- How comfortable am I with using AI for optimization assistance?

- What areas of optimization can AI improve in my workflow?

- How can I ensure AI-driven optimization aligns with project goals?

- What strategies can I use to validate AI suggestions effectively?

- How can AI support my role in maintaining high standards in code quality?

Self-Reflection

- Reflect on initial thoughts about AI in optimization—have they evolved?

- How do you see AI fitting into your optimization workflow going forward?

- Are there aspects of optimization where human oversight is crucial? Why?

- How can AI assist you in becoming more efficient in code improvement?

- What steps can you take to ensure a balanced approach with AI in optimization?

Chapter 12: AI in Collaboration – Enhancing Teamwork or Replacing It?

Chapter 12: AI in Collaboration – Enhancing Teamwork or Replacing It?

The team knew that effective collaboration was key to successful projects. While each member brought unique strengths to the table, their best work came from combining insights, sharing updates, and troubleshooting together. Today, Bob wanted to explore whether Codey could assist in their collaborative workflow, helping them streamline communication, documentation, and version control.

"Alright, team," Bob began, addressing the group. "Today, we're going to see if Codey can support us in collaboration. The idea is to let Codey help us keep track of updates, share code, and even improve our documentation process. It's here to help us stay organized and aligned."

Jordan looked intrigued. "So, Codey is going to act as a kind of virtual assistant, helping us manage our work together?"

"Exactly," Bob replied. "Codey can help with documentation, track changes, and alert us to any code conflicts. It's not a replacement for our team's communication, but it might reduce the friction points in our workflow."

Riley nodded, agreeing. "It sounds useful. Sometimes we spend a lot of time just getting everyone on the same page."

Bob encouraged them, "That's the idea. Let's try using Codey to smooth out some of the collaborative tasks that can slow us down."

Codey's Role in Collaborative Tasks

To give Codey a test run, Bob asked the team to use it to help organize a shared module. They each made updates to the code, then activated Codey to assist with version tracking and documentation. Codey provided real-time support by:

- **Documenting Changes**: Codey tracked each team member's updates and automatically logged changes, creating a clear record of modifications.

- **Identifying Conflicts**: It flagged areas where two team members had made conflicting changes, allowing them to resolve issues before committing.

- **Providing Documentation Suggestions**: Codey suggested summaries for new functions, offering descriptions to standardize documentation across the team.

Pat reviewed the documentation Codey had suggested and was impressed. "It's helpful to have an initial description in place. This saves us time, especially when we're focused on getting the code written."

Jordan agreed. "And the conflict detection is really helpful too. I like that we're catching these issues early instead of when we're about to commit."

Alex, however, was still cautious. "This is useful, but it doesn't replace real collaboration. Codey can track changes, but it doesn't understand why we're making them. We still need to discuss our updates with each other."

Bob nodded. "Exactly, Alex. Codey is here to help with logistics, not to replace our communication. Use it to support collaboration, not to take over our teamwork."

Balancing AI in Collaboration with Direct Communication

As the team continued to use Codey, they noticed both the advantages and limitations of its collaborative support. While Codey's documentation suggestions and conflict alerts saved time, the team still found that real-time discussions were essential to fully understand each other's updates and intentions.

Riley, who valued clear documentation, found Codey's summaries useful as a starting point. "This is great for organizing our work, but we still need to add context to make the documentation truly valuable."

Pat noted, "It's easy to see Codey as a shortcut, but we need to remember that real collaboration comes from shared understanding, not just shared code."

Bob encouraged the team to keep using Codey as a tool, but to stay connected through direct communication. "AI can make collaboration easier, but it's still our discussions, insights, and shared goals that drive our work forward. Let's make sure Codey supports our teamwork, not replaces it."

Guidelines for AI-Assisted Collaboration

After their session, Bob gathered the team to outline best practices for using Codey to enhance their collaborative process, ensuring AI was a support tool rather than a replacement for direct communication.

- **Use AI for Routine Tasks**: Allow Codey to assist with documentation, change tracking, and conflict alerts to streamline collaborative logistics.

- **Prioritize Human Communication**: Rely on direct discussions to ensure clarity and alignment, using Codey's insights as support.

- **Document AI Contributions**: Track where AI-driven documentation and conflict detection were helpful, refining the process over time.

- **Balance Automation with Context**: Use Codey to standardize documentation and identify conflicts, but add personal insights for full context.

- **Encourage Real-Time Collaboration**: Keep direct communication at the center of teamwork, using AI as a support rather than a primary communicator.

"Codey is a great tool for keeping us organized," Bob concluded. "But real collaboration is about understanding, not just sharing files. Let's make sure we're using AI to enhance, not replace, our teamwork."

The team left with a clear understanding of how to integrate Codey into their collaborative process. They felt empowered to use AI as a support system, knowing that their direct communication remained the foundation of their success.

Alex's Notebook

- Codey's tracking and documentation save time, but communication is still key.

- Documenting AI-driven changes keeps track of collaborative logistics.

- Balancing AI with direct discussion ensures clarity and shared goals.

- AI-driven collaboration is efficient, but we still need real teamwork.

- Codey is helpful, but it's not a substitute for team discussions.

Jordan's Notebook

- Codey's tracking and conflict detection streamline our collaborative work.

- Learning from AI's suggestions refines our documentation process.

- Documenting AI-driven changes supports our shared understanding.

- AI makes collaboration feel more organized without replacing teamwork.

- Codey feels like a useful assistant in our collaborative efforts.

Pat's Notebook

- AI-driven documentation and tracking save time on routine tasks.

- Maintaining communication ensures Codey's insights align with our goals.

- Documenting changes supports clarity and long-term collaboration.

- AI assists with logistics but requires real-time discussions for depth.

- Optimistic about AI's role in efficient, organized collaboration.

Riley's Notebook

- Codey's documentation support is helpful but needs added context.

- Maintaining documentation of AI-driven suggestions aids in QA.

- AI can handle routine tasks, freeing us to focus on deeper collaboration.

- Collaboration is smoother with AI as a support, but we still need oversight.

- Cautiously optimistic about AI's role in teamwork.

Bob's Notebook

- AI-driven collaboration improves efficiency but requires oversight.

- Documentation of AI contributions is key to transparency and quality.

- Encouraging the team to balance AI with manual documentation efforts.

- Confident that AI can support collaboration when used thoughtfully.

- The team's shared understanding remains the foundation of collaboration.

Practical Advice

- Use AI tools to assist with routine collaboration tasks, such as documentation and conflict detection.

- Always prioritize direct communication to ensure alignment and shared goals.

- Track AI-driven contributions and document any manual adjustments for future improvement.

- Balance AI-driven organization with direct discussions for comprehensive teamwork.

- Treat AI as a supportive partner in collaboration, relying on human communication to guide its role.

Implementation

- Start by using AI for initial documentation and conflict detection to streamline collaboration.

- Establish protocols for validating and documenting AI-driven collaborative changes.

- Use AI-driven insights to support real-time discussions, maintaining alignment.

- Regularly assess the balance between AI and manual collaboration efforts.

- Encourage continuous improvement to refine AI's role in the collaboration process.

Real-World Insight

In modern development teams, AI tools like Slackbot and GitHub's AI-powered features support collaboration by automating documentation, version control, and conflict detection. These tools help teams streamline communication, reduce errors, and stay organized. However, successful collaboration combines AI's efficiency with direct human discussions, ensuring that shared understanding remains at the core of teamwork.

Pitfalls to Avoid

- Relying solely on AI for collaborative tasks without direct communication.

- Failing to document AI-driven changes, leading to missed insights.

- Allowing AI efficiency to overshadow the need for shared understanding.

- Ignoring project-specific requirements in favor of AI suggestions.

- Neglecting the need for balanced collaboration between AI and human interaction.

Self-Assessment

- How comfortable am I with using AI for collaborative assistance?

- What areas of collaboration can AI improve in my workflow?

- How can I ensure AI-driven documentation aligns with project goals?

- What strategies can I use to validate AI suggestions effectively?

- How can AI support my role in maintaining high standards in teamwork?

Self-Reflection

- Reflect on initial thoughts about AI in collaboration—have they evolved?

- How do you see AI fitting into your collaborative workflow going forward?

- Are there aspects of collaboration where human oversight is crucial? Why?

- How can AI assist you in becoming more efficient in teamwork?

- What steps can you take to ensure a balanced approach with AI in collaboration?

Chapter 13: AI in Testing – Quality Booster or Shortcut to Trouble?

Chapter 13: AI in Testing – Quality Booster or Shortcut to Trouble?

Testing was an integral part of the team's process, helping them catch bugs, validate features, and ensure a high-quality product. While they had incorporated Codey into various aspects of testing before, today Bob wanted to see if Codey could take on a larger role, managing more complex test scenarios and providing additional quality assurance.

"Alright, team," Bob began, gathering everyone's attention. "Today, we're going to try expanding Codey's role in our testing. The goal is to see if it can help us catch issues early, particularly with complex cases that often slip through our initial reviews."

Riley, the team's quality assurance expert, looked intrigued. "So, Codey will be generating tests for more advanced scenarios?"

"That's right," Bob replied. "We'll let Codey handle a mix of edge cases, regression tests, and performance checks. It's not here to replace our judgment, but it might help us cover more ground in less time."

Alex, still skeptical about AI in testing, raised a hand. "But testing isn't just about running scenarios. It's about understanding the application's behavior. Can Codey really anticipate the range of user actions?"

Bob nodded, acknowledging the point. "That's where our oversight comes in. Codey can suggest test cases and check for common issues, but we're responsible for making sure the results align with our quality standards."

Codey's Test Generation and Execution

To give Codey a try, Bob assigned it to analyze a module with complex interactions, asking it to generate a range of test cases. Codey's results included:

- **Edge Case Testing**: Codey identified potential edge cases, such as maximum and minimum input limits, extreme values, and unusual data formats.

- **Regression Testing**: It generated a suite of tests for recent updates, checking that new code hadn't unintentionally affected existing functionality.

- **Performance Testing**: Codey suggested a series of tests to analyze the module's performance under varying loads, helping the team identify potential bottlenecks.

Jordan was impressed by Codey's output. "These are scenarios we might not have thought to test, at least not in the first pass. It's definitely covering a lot of ground."

Riley reviewed the edge cases and found that while some were useful, others needed refinement. "Codey is giving us a good starting point, but some tests need adjustment to match real-world use cases. We can't assume every user will follow the AI's logic."

Bob encouraged the team to use Codey's suggestions as a foundation, adding their insights to create a thorough and practical testing suite. "Think of Codey as a tool to boost our efficiency, but we're still responsible for the final quality."

Balancing AI-Driven Testing with Manual Oversight

As the team tested Codey's generated scenarios, they found that while AI-driven tests covered many basic and routine cases, they lacked the nuance that human testers brought. Some tests generated by Codey didn't fully consider user behavior or the project's specific requirements, which led the team to supplement its insights with manual testing.

Pat appreciated Codey's regression testing, which identified a few unexpected interactions that had gone unnoticed. "This is where Codey is most valuable. It's catching small changes that could have a big impact on functionality."

However, Riley raised a cautionary note. "Codey's tests are thorough but mechanical. It's a great boost for coverage, but it doesn't understand the intention behind each feature. We still need to check that everything aligns with the user experience we want to create."

Bob agreed. "AI can be an incredible support in testing, but it's not a replacement for our insight. Let's use Codey to strengthen our quality control without losing sight of the human perspective."

Guidelines for AI-Assisted Testing

After their session, Bob led the team in establishing guidelines to effectively integrate Codey into their testing workflow. These principles would help them maximize Codey's contributions while maintaining the depth and quality of their testing process.

- **Use AI for Routine Testing**: Allow Codey to handle basic scenarios, regression tests, and edge cases to streamline the testing workload.

- **Validate Complex Test Cases**: Review AI-generated tests for alignment with project goals and adjust them to ensure real-world applicability.

- **Document AI Contributions**: Track where AI-driven tests were used and where manual adjustments were necessary, supporting continuous improvement.

- **Balance Automation with Human Insight**: Use Codey's efficiency to cover more ground but rely on human testing for user behavior and project-specific details.

- **Encourage Comprehensive Coverage**: Apply AI-driven tests as a foundation, supplementing them with manual tests to ensure full quality assurance.

"Codey can help us reach a higher level of quality faster," Bob concluded. "But real quality comes from understanding, and that's something only we can bring. Let's make sure AI supports our standards without lowering them."

The team left the meeting with a deeper appreciation for Codey's role in testing. They knew that AI could streamline their process, but only their expertise could guarantee a high-quality product.

Alex's Notebook

- Codey's testing saves time on basic cases, but validation is key.

- Documenting AI-driven test cases helps track coverage.

- Balancing AI suggestions with practical testing is essential for quality.

- AI-driven testing is efficient, but we still need thorough checks.

- Quality is more than tests; it's understanding user behavior.

Jordan's Notebook

- Codey's edge cases and regression tests streamline testing.

- Learning from AI's testing approach enhances my QA skills.

- Documenting AI-driven changes supports our testing workflow.

- AI adds value, but human testing ensures quality and relevance.

- Codey is a strong partner in our quality efforts.

Pat's Notebook

- AI-driven testing provides broad coverage but needs oversight.

- Maintaining control ensures Codey's tests align with real-world needs.

- Documenting changes aids in future debugging and QA.

- AI assists with routine cases but requires careful validation.

- Optimistic about AI's role in comprehensive, quality-focused testing.

Riley's Notebook

- Codey's test suggestions are helpful but need refinement.

- Documenting AI-driven tests aids in tracking coverage and quality.

- AI can handle routine scenarios, letting us focus on complex testing.

- Testing is smoother with AI as a support, but we still need oversight.

- Cautiously optimistic about AI's role in maintaining quality.

Bob's Notebook

- AI-driven testing provides efficiency but requires validation for quality.

- Documentation of AI contributions is key to transparency and improvement.

- Encouraging the team to balance AI with manual testing efforts.

- Confident that AI can support testing when used thoughtfully.

- The team's expertise remains the foundation of our quality standards.

Practical Advice

- Use AI tools to assist with routine testing, such as edge cases and regression.

- Always validate AI-driven tests to ensure alignment with project requirements.

- Track AI-driven insights and document any modifications for clarity.

- Balance AI-driven efficiency with manual testing for comprehensive quality.

- Treat AI as a supportive partner in testing, using human expertise to guide its role.

Implementation

- Start by using AI for initial testing to cover basic and routine cases.

- Establish protocols for validating and documenting AI-driven test changes.

- Apply AI-driven tests as a foundation, supplementing them with human oversight.

- Regularly assess the balance between AI and manual testing to maintain quality.

- Encourage continuous improvement to refine AI's role in the testing process.

Real-World Insight

AI-driven testing tools, like Testim and Applitools, help companies streamline quality assurance by automating routine and regression tests. These tools reduce the workload for QA teams, allowing them to focus on complex scenarios. However, the best results combine AI-driven efficiency with human oversight to ensure tests align with real-world requirements and user behavior.

Pitfalls to Avoid

- Relying solely on AI for testing without validating suggestions.

- Failing to document AI-driven testing changes, leading to missed insights.

- Allowing AI efficiency to overshadow the need for practical testing.

- Ignoring project-specific requirements in favor of AI-driven tests.

- Neglecting the need for balanced coverage between AI and manual testing.

Self-Assessment

- How comfortable am I with using AI for testing assistance?

- What areas of testing can AI improve in my workflow?

- How can I ensure AI-driven tests align with project requirements?

- What strategies can I use to validate AI suggestions effectively?

- How can AI support my role in maintaining high standards in testing?

Self-Reflection

- Reflect on initial thoughts about AI in testing—have they evolved?

- How do you see AI fitting into your testing workflow going forward?

- Are there aspects of testing where human oversight is crucial? Why?

- How can AI assist you in becoming more efficient in quality assurance?

- What steps can you take to ensure a balanced approach with AI in testing?

Chapter 14: AI in Code Review – Second Set of Eyes or Biased View?

Chapter 14: AI in Code Review – Second Set of Eyes or Biased View?

Code review was one of the team's core practices, an essential step that ensured the quality, consistency, and maintainability of their codebase. While they had already used Codey for basic code checks, Bob wanted to test whether Codey could serve as a more involved "second set of eyes" in the review process, providing deeper insights and helping them identify issues faster.

"Today, we're going to lean on Codey a bit more in code review," Bob announced. "The idea is to see if Codey can help us catch issues we might miss and suggest improvements beyond just syntax corrections."

Jordan looked intrigued. "So, we're treating Codey more like an actual reviewer?"

"Exactly," Bob replied. "But remember, it's still AI. We're here to catch the nuances, while Codey's role is to highlight potential issues and provide a starting point for our discussions."

Alex, who was cautious about AI in reviews, raised a question. "But if we rely on Codey too much, could it introduce biases? AI might over-prioritize certain types of issues and overlook others."

"That's a valid concern," Bob acknowledged. "Codey can't fully understand project-specific goals or design choices. Our job is to balance its suggestions with our judgment, ensuring nothing important slips through."

Codey's Code Review Process

To see how Codey could assist, Bob selected a complex module for review, enabling Codey to analyze the code and provide a list of recommendations. Within moments, Codey highlighted several areas:

- **Code Consistency**: Codey flagged lines where naming conventions and formatting didn't align with the team's standards, suggesting adjustments for clarity.

- **Logic Enhancements**: It identified areas where code could be simplified or optimized, proposing refactored versions to improve readability and performance.

- **Security Considerations**: Codey noted potential vulnerabilities, recommending stricter access controls and suggesting ways to sanitize user inputs.

Chapter 14: AI in Code Review – Second Set of Eyes or Biased View?

Pat reviewed the recommendations and was impressed. "Codey is thorough, especially with consistency and security checks. It's like having an extra layer of quality control."

Jordan agreed. "These suggestions save time on the basics, letting us focus more on the architecture and functionality."

However, Riley pointed out an important limitation. "Codey flagged a few areas that don't really need changing. It doesn't fully understand the intent behind every line of code."

Bob nodded. "That's why we're here. Codey provides insights, but it's up to us to decide if they're relevant. Let's treat Codey's feedback as a guide, not a mandate."

Balancing AI-Driven Review with Human Judgment

As the team worked through Codey's feedback, they quickly recognized that while AI-driven reviews provided valuable suggestions, they needed careful validation. Codey's formatting and naming checks were helpful in maintaining consistency, but certain refactoring suggestions conflicted with the project's design goals. Additionally, Codey's security recommendations, though thorough, required additional context to determine their relevance.

Alex, who was initially skeptical, admitted that Codey's review process had been helpful in catching small but important details. "It's catching a lot of things we'd normally address in the second pass. This frees us up to focus on the bigger picture."

However, he remained cautious. "But Codey's suggestions still lack nuance. We have to make sure we're not just accepting its feedback without evaluating the impact."

Bob encouraged the team to use Codey's suggestions as a starting point, applying their expertise to finalize the review. "This is where balance is key. Codey gives us efficiency, but only we can bring the depth."

Guidelines for AI-Assisted Code Review

After the code review session, Bob led a discussion to outline best practices for integrating Codey into their code review process, ensuring that AI-driven insights enhanced rather than replaced human judgment.

- **Use AI for Routine Checks**: Allow Codey to handle consistency, security, and performance checks, streamlining basic review tasks.

- **Validate AI Recommendations**: Review each AI suggestion to ensure it aligns with project-specific goals and design choices.

- **Document AI Contributions**: Track where AI-driven feedback led to actual changes and where adjustments were necessary to clarify Codey's role.

- **Balance Automation with Contextual Insight**: Use Codey's efficiency to cover routine checks but rely on human insight for functionality and design intent.

- **Encourage Critical Review**: Apply Codey's suggestions as a guide, validating each recommendation to ensure comprehensive and relevant code quality.

"Codey can help us review code faster, but the final quality depends on us," Bob concluded. "Let's make sure AI supports our standards without diluting them. Every line we accept or reject is a decision that reflects our expertise."

The team left the meeting with a renewed perspective on using AI in code review. They saw Codey not as a replacement but as an invaluable support, one that enhanced their process without compromising the standards they'd worked hard to establish.

Alex's Notebook

- Codey's review suggestions streamline basic checks, but oversight is key.

- Documenting AI-driven changes supports transparency in our workflow.

- Balancing AI suggestions with design intent ensures quality.

- AI-driven review is efficient, but we need to verify each recommendation.

- Quality is more than checks; it's about aligning with project goals.

Jordan's Notebook

- Codey's consistency checks speed up our review process.

- Learning from AI's review approach refines my own reviewing skills.

- Documenting AI contributions helps track its role in our workflow.

- AI makes code review feel less daunting, saving us time.

- Codey is a strong partner in our quality assurance efforts.

Pat's Notebook

- AI-driven review provides valuable insights but needs context-specific validation.

- Maintaining control ensures Codey's suggestions align with our standards.

- Documenting changes supports clarity and accountability.

- AI assists with routine review tasks but requires careful oversight.

- Optimistic about AI's role in comprehensive, quality-focused review.

Riley's Notebook

- Codey's review suggestions are helpful but need refinement.

- Maintaining documentation of AI-driven changes aids in quality assurance.

- AI can handle routine checks, letting us focus on complex review needs.

- Code review is smoother with AI as a support, but we still need oversight.

- Cautiously optimistic about AI's role in maintaining code quality.

Bob's Notebook

- AI-driven code review improves efficiency but requires critical oversight.

- Documentation of AI contributions is key to transparency and quality.

- Encouraging the team to balance AI with manual review efforts.

- Confident that AI can support code review when used thoughtfully.

- The team's expertise remains the foundation of our code quality.

Practical Advice

- Use AI tools to assist with routine code review tasks, such as consistency and security checks.

- Always validate AI-driven suggestions to ensure alignment with project goals.

- Track AI-driven insights and document any modifications for future improvement.

- Balance AI-driven efficiency with manual review for comprehensive quality.

- Treat AI as a supportive partner in code review, using human insight to guide its role.

Implementation

- Start by using AI for initial code review to catch consistency and security issues.

- Establish protocols for validating and documenting AI-driven review changes.

- Use AI-driven insights to support manual review, focusing on critical areas.

- Regularly assess the balance between AI and manual review to maintain quality.

- Encourage continuous improvement to refine AI's role in the review process.

Real-World Insight

AI-driven code review tools, such as SonarQube and Codacy, help companies streamline quality assurance by automating consistency, security, and performance checks. These tools reduce the review workload, allowing developers to focus on functionality and design. However, successful code review combines AI-driven efficiency with human oversight to ensure that the code aligns with project goals and standards.

Pitfalls to Avoid

- Relying solely on AI for code review without manual validation.

- Failing to document AI-driven review changes, leading to missed insights.

- Allowing AI efficiency to overshadow the need for contextual review.

- Ignoring project-specific requirements in favor of AI-driven checks.

- Neglecting the need for balanced review between AI and human interaction.

Self-Assessment

- How comfortable am I with using AI for code review assistance?

- What areas of code review can AI improve in my workflow?

- How can I ensure AI-driven review aligns with project requirements?

- What strategies can I use to validate AI suggestions effectively?

- How can AI support my role in maintaining high standards in code review?

Self-Reflection

- Reflect on initial thoughts about AI in code review—have they evolved?

- How do you see AI fitting into your review workflow going forward?

- Are there aspects of code review where human oversight is crucial? Why?

- How can AI assist you in becoming more efficient in quality assurance?

- What steps can you take to ensure a balanced approach with AI in code review?

Chapter 15: AI in Documentation – Helpful Guide or Confusing Addition?

Chapter 15: AI in Documentation – Helpful Guide or Confusing Addition?

Documentation was an often-overlooked but critical part of the team's workflow. Proper documentation meant that code was easier to understand, maintain, and improve upon down the road. Today, Bob wanted to explore how Codey could assist the team in making documentation more consistent, complete, and efficient.

"Today, we're going to see how Codey can help us with our documentation process," Bob began, addressing the group. "Our goal is to streamline documentation, ensuring that our code is well-documented and easy to follow without taking up too much of our time."

Riley looked intrigued. "So, Codey is going to auto-generate parts of our documentation? Like summaries or function descriptions?"

"Exactly," Bob replied. "Codey can suggest descriptions, highlight dependencies, and provide a starting point. We'll still need to refine its output, but this might help us establish a more consistent baseline."

Jordan looked excited. "If Codey can handle the basics, it could free us up to focus on documenting more complex parts."

"Right," Bob agreed. "But let's remember: Codey can't capture intent or specific project nuances. It's here to help us get started, but the quality of our documentation still depends on us."

Codey's Documentation Support

To give Codey a try, Bob selected a module with limited documentation and asked the team to use Codey's assistance to generate descriptions and summaries. Codey's initial output included:

- **Function Summaries**: Codey provided short descriptions for each function, explaining its purpose and expected input/output parameters.

- **Dependency Notes**: It identified dependencies between functions and modules, helping the team track connections within the codebase.

- **Usage Examples**: Codey generated simple usage examples for key functions, demonstrating basic functionality for future reference.

Riley reviewed the function summaries and was impressed by the level of detail. "These are actually pretty useful. Codey is giving us a head start on the descriptions, saving us time on the initial drafts."

Chapter 15: AI in Documentation – Helpful Guide or Confusing Addition?

Pat agreed, noting the usefulness of the dependency notes. "This really helps with organizing our thoughts. Knowing which functions rely on each other gives us a clearer picture for documentation."

However, Alex was more cautious. "Codey's descriptions are solid, but they're generic. They miss the nuances of why we implemented things the way we did. We'll need to add more context."

Bob nodded. "Exactly. Codey can get us part of the way there, but we need to add the project-specific information that only we understand. Let's treat these AI-generated descriptions as starting points."

Balancing AI-Generated Documentation with Human Clarity

As the team worked through Codey's documentation suggestions, they discovered that while AI-driven descriptions provided a helpful foundation, they often needed additional context to ensure they were clear and useful. Codey's summaries and examples saved time on basic documentation, but the team still had to add clarifying details and explanations that only they could provide.

Jordan found the usage examples especially helpful. "These examples give a quick overview of how each function works. They're not perfect, but they're good enough to build on."

However, Riley pointed out a limitation. "Codey's documentation lacks the 'why' behind each function. Without understanding the purpose, future developers might not fully grasp our choices."

Bob encouraged the team to use Codey's documentation as a framework, adding their expertise to ensure clarity and completeness. "Documentation is as much about clarity as it is about accuracy. Codey can handle the basics, but we're the ones who ensure it's meaningful."

Guidelines for AI-Assisted Documentation

After the session, Bob led a discussion to establish best practices for integrating Codey into their documentation workflow, ensuring AI-driven insights enhanced clarity without sacrificing context.

- **Use AI for Routine Descriptions**: Allow Codey to generate basic descriptions, dependency notes, and usage examples, streamlining the initial drafting process.

- **Validate and Refine AI-Generated Content**: Review each AI-generated description to add necessary context, ensuring alignment with the project's goals and design.

- **Document AI Contributions**: Track where AI-generated documentation was helpful and where manual additions were made, supporting transparency.

- **Balance Automation with Human Insight**: Use AI to cover routine descriptions but rely on the team to add clarity and explain intent.

- **Encourage Consistency**: Apply Codey's documentation framework as a baseline, building consistency in style while adding meaningful details.

"Codey can make our documentation faster and more consistent," Bob concluded. "But true clarity comes from us. Let's make sure AI enhances our documentation without diluting the meaning."

The team left the meeting with a clear understanding of how to leverage Codey in their documentation process. They knew that AI could streamline the basics, but only their expertise could ensure clarity and context, creating documentation that was as useful as it was comprehensive.

Alex's Notebook

- Codey's documentation saves time on basic descriptions, but oversight is key.

- Documenting AI-driven contributions keeps track of its role.

- Balancing AI suggestions with project context ensures meaningful documentation.

- AI-driven documentation is efficient, but we need to refine it.

- Quality documentation requires explaining both how and why.

Jordan's Notebook

- Codey's initial descriptions and examples streamline documentation.

- Learning from AI's approach helps improve my own documentation skills.

- Documenting AI contributions helps maintain consistency in style.

- AI adds value, but human clarification ensures relevance.

- Codey feels like a helpful assistant in our documentation efforts.

Pat's Notebook

- AI-driven documentation provides a good starting point but needs context.
- Maintaining control ensures descriptions align with our project goals.
- Documenting changes supports clarity and long-term maintainability.
- AI assists with routine descriptions but requires careful validation.
- Optimistic about AI's role in consistent, efficient documentation.

Riley's Notebook

- Codey's summaries are helpful but lack intent behind functions.
- Maintaining documentation of AI-driven content aids in quality.
- AI can handle routine descriptions, letting us focus on context.
- Documentation is smoother with AI as a support, but we still need oversight.
- Cautiously optimistic about AI's role in creating useful documentation.

Bob's Notebook

- AI-driven documentation improves efficiency but requires critical oversight.
- Documentation of AI contributions is key to transparency and clarity.
- Encouraging the team to balance AI with manual additions.
- Confident that AI can support documentation when used thoughtfully.
- The team's insights remain the foundation of meaningful documentation.

Practical Advice

- Use AI tools to assist with routine documentation tasks, such as function descriptions and dependency notes.

- Always validate AI-driven descriptions to ensure they align with project context.

- Track AI-driven insights and document any manual modifications for clarity.

- Balance AI-driven efficiency with human insight for comprehensive documentation.

- Treat AI as a supportive partner in documentation, using human expertise to guide its role.

Implementation

- Start by using AI for initial documentation to cover basic function summaries and dependencies.

- Establish protocols for validating and documenting AI-driven content.

- Apply AI-driven documentation as a foundation, adding project-specific context for clarity.

- Regularly assess the balance between AI and manual documentation to maintain quality.

- Encourage consistency by using AI as a style guide for standard documentation.

Real-World Insight

AI-driven documentation tools like Doxygen and GitHub's Copilot are widely used in software development to create standardized descriptions and dependency tracking. These tools allow developers to streamline routine documentation, saving time for more complex explanations. However, successful documentation combines AI's efficiency with human insight, ensuring clarity and context for maintainability.

Pitfalls to Avoid

- Relying solely on AI for documentation without adding context.

- Failing to document AI-driven changes, leading to missed insights.

- Allowing AI efficiency to overshadow the need for comprehensive explanations.

- Ignoring project-specific requirements in favor of AI-driven descriptions.

- Neglecting the need for balanced documentation between AI and human input.

Self-Assessment

- How comfortable am I with using AI for documentation assistance?

- What areas of documentation can AI improve in my workflow?

- How can I ensure AI-driven documentation aligns with project requirements?

- What strategies can I use to validate AI suggestions effectively?

- How can AI support my role in maintaining high standards in documentation?

Self-Reflection

- Reflect on initial thoughts about AI in documentation—have they evolved?

- How do you see AI fitting into your documentation workflow going forward?

- Are there aspects of documentation where human oversight is crucial? Why?

- How can AI assist you in becoming more efficient in creating meaningful documentation?

- What steps can you take to ensure a balanced approach with AI in documentation?

Chapter 16: AI in Team Dynamics – Uniting Teams or Driving Them Apart?

Chapter 16: AI in Team Dynamics – Uniting Teams or Driving Them Apart?

Since Codey's integration into their workflow, the team had experienced changes—some subtle, others more pronounced—in the way they collaborated and communicated. Bob realized that as they relied more on Codey, it was essential to address how AI was influencing their team dynamics. Today, he wanted the team to reflect on how AI affected their roles, responsibilities, and sense of collaboration.

"Alright, team," Bob began, gathering everyone's attention. "Today, I want us to focus on something less technical but equally important: how Codey is changing the way we work together."

Jordan, always enthusiastic, was the first to respond. "I think Codey's made us more efficient. We're catching issues faster and working through routine tasks quicker."

"That's true," Bob agreed, "but I want us to dig deeper. Has AI changed the way we see our roles? Or the way we communicate? These are the kinds of questions I want us to consider."

Riley looked thoughtful. "It's definitely affected my role in QA. With Codey handling a lot of the basics, I'm focusing more on complex testing scenarios. But sometimes, I wonder if relying too much on Codey means I'm missing out on parts of the process."

Pat nodded. "Same here. It's like we're being pushed into more specialized roles because Codey's taking over certain tasks. That's good for productivity, but it also means we're each doing less of the overall work."

Codey's Role in Team Dynamics

To facilitate the discussion, Bob asked the team to share specific ways Codey had influenced their collaboration and individual responsibilities. The team's insights were varied, reflecting both the benefits and the potential challenges of integrating AI into their workflow:

- **Increased Efficiency**: Many team members agreed that Codey improved efficiency, allowing them to focus on higher-level tasks instead of repetitive work.

- **Shifted Roles**: With AI handling routine tasks, some team members felt their roles had shifted, becoming more specialized as Codey took on broader responsibilities.

- **Reduced Communication**: Because Codey managed certain documentation and tracking, the team found they communicated less about basic tasks, which could affect their overall cohesion.

- **Role Ambiguity**: Some team members expressed concerns about overlapping roles, especially as AI blurred the lines between responsibilities.

Alex voiced a common concern. "Sometimes I feel like we're each just handing off tasks to Codey without really discussing it. We used to talk through each step, but now it's more automated. I'm worried we might be losing the collaboration that made us effective in the first place."

Bob nodded, acknowledging the point. "That's a valid concern. AI can help with efficiency, but we have to make sure we're not losing sight of our team's synergy. Let's think about ways to keep the best of both worlds."

Balancing AI with Team Communication and Cohesion

As they continued the discussion, the team brainstormed ways to maintain strong collaboration even as they integrated more AI-driven tasks. Riley suggested weekly check-ins focused specifically on team dynamics, where they could discuss how Codey's role was affecting their workflow.

"I think it would help us stay connected and catch any issues early on," Riley said. "If we're open about how we're feeling, we can keep AI from driving us apart."

Pat agreed. "It might also help to define which tasks we want to keep human-led versus AI-led. If we clarify our roles, we can avoid role ambiguity and make sure we're all on the same page."

Bob encouraged them. "That's exactly the direction we should take. AI is a tool, but our teamwork is what drives our success. Let's make sure Codey enhances our dynamics instead of creating distance."

Guidelines for Maintaining Team Cohesion with AI

After the discussion, Bob led the team in creating guidelines to ensure Codey supported rather than hindered their team dynamics. These principles would help them maintain open communication, clear roles, and a collaborative spirit, even as AI played a larger role in their workflow.

- **Use AI to Support, Not Replace, Communication**: Encourage regular discussions about tasks, using Codey to enhance but not substitute direct communication.

- **Define Human-Led and AI-Led Tasks**: Clarify which responsibilities will remain human-led to ensure everyone understands their role and contributions.

- **Regularly Assess Team Dynamics**: Schedule check-ins to discuss how AI is affecting team collaboration and address any concerns that arise.

- **Foster Role Clarity**: Use Codey to support roles but ensure that responsibilities are clearly defined to avoid ambiguity.

- **Encourage Team Cohesion**: Promote practices that keep the team connected, focusing on the human aspects of collaboration and shared goals.

"Codey is a powerful tool, but our teamwork is the real magic here," Bob concluded. "AI should support our roles, not redefine them. Let's keep our communication strong and make sure Codey enhances, not replaces, the way we work together."

The team left the meeting with a renewed understanding of how to balance AI with collaboration. They knew that while Codey could make them more efficient, it was their shared commitment and open communication that made their work meaningful and cohesive.

Alex's Notebook

- Codey improves efficiency, but we need to ensure it doesn't replace collaboration.

- Regular communication about AI's role keeps our team connected.

- Balancing AI with human-led tasks ensures clear roles and responsibilities.

- AI-driven efficiency is great, but we can't lose our team dynamic.

- Teamwork is as much about connection as it is about productivity.

Jordan's Notebook

- Codey's support allows us to focus on complex tasks, improving productivity.

- Learning to define human-led tasks keeps roles clear and avoids ambiguity.

- Regular check-ins about team dynamics help us stay connected.

- AI assists our workflow, but we need direct communication for cohesion.

- Codey is a helpful tool, but human teamwork drives success.

Pat's Notebook

- AI-driven efficiency streamlines workflow, but clarity in roles is essential.

- Keeping regular check-ins ensures AI supports rather than divides our team.

- Documenting human-led and AI-led tasks keeps roles consistent.

- AI is helpful, but we still need team collaboration to stay cohesive.

- Optimistic about AI's role in enhancing teamwork with clear boundaries.

Riley's Notebook

- Codey's support in routine tasks is helpful, but we need role clarity.

- Maintaining documentation of human and AI tasks aids in accountability.

- AI can support routine work, letting us focus on higher-level collaboration.

- Teamwork is smoother with AI as a support, but we still need communication.

- Cautiously optimistic about AI's role in supporting team dynamics.

Bob's Notebook

- AI-driven support enhances workflow but requires clear role boundaries.

- Documentation of AI and human tasks is key to transparency and cohesion.

- Encouraging regular team check-ins to balance AI with collaboration.

- Confident that AI can support team dynamics when used thoughtfully.

- The team's connection and open communication remain foundational.

Practical Advice

- Use AI to support routine tasks, but prioritize regular team discussions for cohesion.

- Define human-led and AI-led tasks to maintain clarity in roles and responsibilities.

- Track AI-driven contributions and document any task adjustments to clarify roles.

- Balance AI-driven efficiency with human collaboration for comprehensive team cohesion.

- Treat AI as a supportive partner, using human oversight to maintain strong team dynamics.

Implementation

- Start by using AI for routine tasks, freeing up time for higher-level collaboration.

- Establish protocols for validating AI-driven tasks and document role definitions.

- Schedule regular check-ins to discuss team dynamics and how AI is affecting collaboration.

- Regularly assess the balance between AI and human-led roles to ensure quality.

- Encourage continuous improvement to refine AI's role in supporting teamwork.

Real-World Insight

AI integration in team workflows is growing across industries, with tools like Asana and Slack AI offering collaboration support that automates routine tasks, tracks changes, and standardizes documentation. However, teams that rely too heavily on AI may lose the cohesion and clarity that comes from direct communication and shared responsibilities. Successful AI integration balances efficiency with open, collaborative dynamics.

Pitfalls to Avoid

- Relying solely on AI for collaborative tasks without human communication.
- Failing to document AI-driven tasks, leading to role ambiguity.
- Allowing AI efficiency to overshadow the need for clear roles and teamwork.
- Ignoring team dynamics and project-specific requirements in favor of AI-led solutions.
- Neglecting the need for balanced team collaboration between AI and human input.

Self-Assessment

- How comfortable am I with using AI for collaborative support?
- What areas of team dynamics can AI improve in our workflow?
- How can I ensure AI-driven tasks align with team goals and responsibilities?
- What strategies can I use to validate AI's role in supporting team cohesion?
- How can AI support my role in maintaining high standards in team collaboration?

Self-Reflection

- Reflect on initial thoughts about AI in team dynamics—have they evolved?
- How do you see AI fitting into your collaborative workflow going forward?
- Are there aspects of team dynamics where human oversight is crucial? Why?
- How can AI assist you in enhancing team cohesion and efficiency?

Chapter 16: AI in Team Dynamics – Uniting Teams or Driving Them Apart?

- What steps can you take to ensure a balanced approach with AI in team dynamics?

Chapter 17: AI in Maintenance – Key to Longevity or Temporary Fix?

Chapter 17: AI in Maintenance – Key to Longevity or Temporary Fix?

Maintenance was an ongoing challenge for the team, especially as their projects grew more complex and their codebase expanded. Keeping the code functioning smoothly, identifying areas that required updates, and making improvements without introducing new issues were essential to the team's long-term success. Today, Bob wanted to see how Codey could assist in their maintenance efforts, providing support while allowing the team to focus on strategic improvements.

"Today, we're going to test Codey's role in maintenance," Bob began, addressing the group. "We'll see if AI can help us with routine upkeep—finding outdated code, flagging potential issues, and suggesting optimizations that can extend our codebase's longevity."

Jordan looked intrigued. "So, Codey will help us keep our code healthy, catching issues before they become major problems?"

"That's the idea," Bob replied. "But remember, maintenance is as much about proactive planning as it is about quick fixes. Codey can handle some of the basics, but we still need to take a long-term approach."

Pat, who had experience managing large-scale codebases, nodded in agreement. "AI is useful for handling routine tasks, but maintenance also means knowing when to refactor, when to optimize, and when to update dependencies. It requires both strategy and oversight."

Codey's Role in Routine Maintenance

To give Codey a trial run, Bob selected a section of their codebase that had known issues with outdated code and dependencies. He asked Codey to analyze the code for potential improvements and maintenance suggestions. Codey's initial findings included:

- **Outdated Dependencies**: Codey flagged libraries and frameworks that had newer versions available, recommending updates to avoid compatibility issues.

- **Redundant Code Blocks**: It identified repetitive code that could be consolidated or simplified, potentially reducing maintenance overhead.

- **Optimization Suggestions**: Codey recommended changes to improve memory usage and processing efficiency, ensuring smoother performance over time.

Riley reviewed Codey's suggestions and was impressed. "This is great for catching the small things that can add up over time. Updating dependencies is something we sometimes overlook until it causes issues."

Jordan agreed, finding the consolidation suggestions particularly helpful. "Codey's highlighting areas we might not have noticed. These changes could help keep our codebase clean and more manageable."

However, Alex voiced a common concern. "Updating dependencies and refactoring code can be risky. If we aren't careful, we might introduce new issues, especially if we rely on AI suggestions without fully validating them."

Bob nodded, understanding the concern. "That's why we need to approach Codey's suggestions with caution. Maintenance is about stability as much as improvement. Let's use Codey's recommendations as a starting point, but we're the ones responsible for ensuring our changes are sustainable."

Balancing AI-Driven Maintenance with Long-Term Strategy

As the team worked through Codey's suggestions, they found that while the AI-driven recommendations helped address routine issues, more complex decisions required their expertise. Codey's suggestions for dependency updates, for instance, needed thorough testing to avoid compatibility problems, while some optimization recommendations required fine-tuning to align with the project's goals.

Pat appreciated Codey's help with redundant code blocks, which allowed the team to streamline certain functions without spending hours manually reviewing them. "This is a big help for keeping the code manageable. But we still need to think about long-term structure and usability."

Riley added, "Codey is handling the surface-level maintenance, but strategic maintenance—thinking about future scalability, modularity, and flexibility—is something only we can do."

Bob encouraged the team to view Codey's role as supportive rather than prescriptive, using its insights to improve efficiency while maintaining a long-term approach to code stability. "AI can make maintenance easier, but it's our responsibility to ensure longevity. Let's use Codey as a tool, but let our strategic judgment guide our decisions."

Guidelines for AI-Assisted Maintenance

After their session, Bob led the team in establishing best practices for integrating Codey into their maintenance process, ensuring that AI-driven maintenance supported their long-term strategy without compromising stability.

- **Use AI for Routine Maintenance**: Allow Codey to handle routine tasks like updating dependencies, identifying redundancies, and suggesting optimizations.

- **Validate Complex Changes**: Review AI-driven maintenance suggestions for alignment with project goals, thoroughly testing any changes to ensure stability.

- **Document AI Contributions**: Track where AI-driven maintenance was applied and where manual adjustments were made, providing a record for future reference.

- **Balance Automation with Strategic Planning**: Use AI to streamline routine maintenance, but rely on human insight for decisions affecting scalability and flexibility.

- **Encourage Proactive Maintenance**: Apply AI-driven maintenance as a foundation, combining it with a proactive, strategic approach to ensure long-term code quality.

"Codey can help us stay on top of maintenance, but the real key to longevity is proactive planning," Bob concluded. "Let's use AI as an ally in routine upkeep, but let's also keep our focus on the bigger picture."

The team left the meeting with a renewed commitment to balancing AI-driven maintenance with strategic planning. They knew that while Codey could handle routine tasks, it was their expertise and vision that would keep the codebase strong and sustainable over time.

Alex's Notebook

- Codey's maintenance suggestions streamline routine tasks, but oversight is crucial.

- Documenting AI-driven changes supports transparency in our maintenance process.

- Balancing AI suggestions with strategic planning ensures sustainable improvements.

- AI-driven maintenance is efficient, but we need to focus on long-term stability.

- Maintenance is more than updates; it's about future-proofing.

Jordan's Notebook

- Codey's routine maintenance suggestions save time and help keep code clean.

- Learning from AI's approach refines my understanding of effective maintenance.

- Documenting AI contributions aids in tracking long-term maintenance.

- AI adds value, but human planning ensures future flexibility.

- Codey is a helpful assistant in our maintenance efforts.

Pat's Notebook

- AI-driven maintenance provides a good starting point but needs strategic oversight.

- Maintaining control ensures Codey's suggestions align with project goals.

- Documenting changes supports clarity and accountability.

- AI assists with routine upkeep but requires careful validation for longevity.

- Optimistic about AI's role in proactive, efficient maintenance.

Riley's Notebook

- Codey's maintenance suggestions are helpful but need refinement.

- Maintaining documentation of AI-driven content aids in tracking stability.

- AI can handle routine issues, letting us focus on complex maintenance.

- Maintenance is smoother with AI as a support, but we still need strategic input.

- Cautiously optimistic about AI's role in maintaining code longevity.

Bob's Notebook

- AI-driven maintenance improves efficiency but requires critical oversight.

- Documentation of AI contributions is key to transparency and clarity.

- Encouraging the team to balance AI with proactive maintenance efforts.

- Confident that AI can support long-term stability when used thoughtfully.

- The team's strategic vision remains the foundation of lasting quality.

Practical Advice

- Use AI tools to assist with routine maintenance tasks, such as updating dependencies and identifying redundancies.

- Always validate AI-driven maintenance suggestions to ensure they align with project goals.

- Track AI-driven insights and document any modifications for future improvement.

- Balance AI-driven efficiency with strategic maintenance for comprehensive quality.

- Treat AI as a supportive partner in maintenance, using human insight to guide long-term planning.

Implementation

- Start by using AI for routine maintenance tasks, covering basics like updates and optimizations.

- Establish protocols for validating and documenting AI-driven maintenance changes.

- Apply AI-driven maintenance as a foundation, supplementing it with proactive planning for scalability and flexibility.

- Regularly assess the balance between AI and manual maintenance to ensure quality.

- Encourage continuous improvement to refine AI's role in supporting long-term maintenance.

Real-World Insight

AI-driven maintenance tools, such as WhiteSource and Renovate, help companies streamline code upkeep by automating dependency updates, identifying redundancies, and suggesting optimizations. These tools reduce the workload for developers, allowing them to focus on strategic improvements. However, successful maintenance combines AI's efficiency with human planning, ensuring code quality aligns with long-term goals.

Pitfalls to Avoid

- Relying solely on AI for maintenance without validating suggestions.

- Failing to document AI-driven maintenance changes, leading to missed insights.

- Allowing AI efficiency to overshadow the need for strategic planning.

- Ignoring project-specific requirements in favor of AI-driven updates.

- Neglecting the need for balanced maintenance between AI and human input.

Self-Assessment

- How comfortable am I with using AI for maintenance assistance?

- What areas of maintenance can AI improve in my workflow?

- How can I ensure AI-driven maintenance aligns with project goals?

- What strategies can I use to validate AI suggestions effectively?

- How can AI support my role in maintaining high standards in long-term maintenance?

Self-Reflection

- Reflect on initial thoughts about AI in maintenance—have they evolved?

- How do you see AI fitting into your maintenance workflow going forward?

- Are there aspects of maintenance where human oversight is crucial? Why?

- How can AI assist you in becoming more efficient in proactive maintenance?

- What steps can you take to ensure a balanced approach with AI in maintenance?

Chapter 18: AI in Scaling Up – Growth Catalyst or Bottleneck?

Chapter 18: AI in Scaling Up – Growth Catalyst or Bottleneck?

Scaling up their projects was both a goal and a challenge for the team. With more users, complex features, and an ever-growing codebase, they needed to ensure that their systems could handle increased demands without sacrificing performance or stability. Bob wanted to see if Codey could help support their growth, easing the transition from a small project to a scalable platform capable of meeting long-term goals.

"Today, we're going to explore how Codey can support us in scaling up," Bob began. "Our aim is to use AI to help manage increased loads, monitor performance, and maintain efficiency as our projects expand."

Jordan looked enthusiastic. "So, Codey will help us handle the growing pains of scaling up? That would be a game-changer!"

"Exactly," Bob replied. "But remember, while AI can help us address certain challenges, scaling requires a strategic approach. We need to ensure that Codey's assistance doesn't introduce new bottlenecks as we grow."

Pat, who had experience working on large-scale systems, nodded in agreement. "AI can assist with certain tasks, but scaling up requires planning for complexity, anticipating risks, and ensuring the system remains adaptable. Relying too heavily on AI could create dependencies we didn't anticipate."

Codey's Role in Supporting Growth

To see how Codey could assist in scaling up, Bob assigned it to analyze a module with increased load demands and performance requirements. Codey's initial suggestions included:

- **Load Balancing**: Codey recommended distributing traffic across multiple instances to manage load, ensuring the system could handle higher user demands without overloading.

- **Resource Allocation**: It suggested adjustments to optimize memory usage and processing power, recommending which processes could benefit from dedicated resources.

- **Performance Monitoring**: Codey proposed setting up automated monitoring for key performance indicators (KPIs) to track and flag potential bottlenecks early.

Riley reviewed Codey's load-balancing recommendations, impressed by the AI's ability to identify potential load distribution issues. "This is useful. Codey's suggestions could help us avoid performance issues that often come with scaling."

Chapter 18: AI in Scaling Up – Growth Catalyst or Bottleneck?

Jordan found the resource allocation tips particularly helpful. "If we can manage our resources better, we can scale more efficiently and avoid wasting processing power."

However, Alex pointed out an important consideration. "Automated monitoring and resource allocation are great, but scaling up also means planning for future growth. Codey's suggestions are immediate solutions, but we need to think long-term."

Bob encouraged the team to use Codey's insights as a foundation, applying their expertise to build a scalable system. "Codey can help us manage today's demands, but we're responsible for planning for tomorrow. Let's make sure AI supports our growth without creating new limitations."

Balancing AI-Driven Scaling with Strategic Planning

As the team implemented Codey's suggestions, they found that while AI-driven recommendations provided valuable solutions for current needs, they needed additional planning to ensure the system remained scalable. Codey's load-balancing suggestions were helpful, but they realized that more complex requirements, such as failover strategies and redundancy, required human oversight to anticipate future challenges.

Pat appreciated Codey's automated monitoring setup, which allowed the team to focus on high-priority areas while keeping an eye on system performance. "It's nice to know that we can catch potential issues before they become big problems. But as we scale, monitoring alone won't be enough—we need to plan for resilience."

Riley added, "Codey is helping us with the immediate demands of scaling, but we also need to design our system to handle even greater loads down the line."

Bob reminded the team that scaling up required both short-term and long-term thinking, blending AI efficiency with strategic foresight. "AI can be a great catalyst for growth, but it's up to us to ensure that growth is sustainable. Let's use Codey as a tool, not a crutch, and build a system that supports our goals well into the future."

Guidelines for AI-Assisted Scaling

After their session, Bob led the team in establishing best practices for integrating Codey into their scaling process, ensuring that AI-driven insights complemented rather than replaced strategic planning for growth.

- **Use AI for Immediate Scaling Needs**: Allow Codey to handle routine scaling tasks, such as load balancing, resource allocation, and performance monitoring.

- **Plan for Long-Term Growth**: Use AI-driven insights as a foundation, but apply human expertise to design for resilience, failover, and redundancy.

- **Document AI Contributions**: Track where AI-driven scaling solutions were applied and where manual adjustments were necessary, ensuring transparency and foresight.

- **Balance Efficiency with Adaptability**: Rely on AI to support immediate scaling needs, but ensure the system remains flexible to adapt to future demands.

- **Encourage Proactive Scaling**: Apply AI-driven scaling solutions as part of a larger, proactive strategy for growth, anticipating potential bottlenecks and planning for sustainable scalability.

"Codey can help us scale up, but sustainable growth is something only we can plan for," Bob concluded. "Let's make sure we're building a system that grows with us, not one that limits us. AI should support our ambitions, not define them."

The team left the meeting with a clear understanding of how to integrate Codey into their scaling strategy. They knew that while AI could address immediate scaling challenges, it was their expertise and foresight that would ensure their projects grew sustainably over time.

Alex's Notebook

- Codey's scaling suggestions address immediate needs, but oversight is crucial.

- Documenting AI-driven scaling supports transparency in our growth process.

- Balancing AI suggestions with long-term planning ensures sustainable scalability.

- AI-driven scaling is efficient, but we need to focus on future flexibility.

- Scaling up is more than growth; it's about building for resilience.

Jordan's Notebook

- Codey's scaling suggestions save time on routine scaling tasks.
- Learning from AI's approach refines my understanding of efficient scaling.
- Documenting AI contributions helps track scalability for future planning.
- AI adds value, but human planning ensures long-term adaptability.
- Codey is a helpful assistant in our scaling efforts.

Pat's Notebook

- AI-driven scaling provides a good starting point but needs strategic oversight.
- Maintaining control ensures Codey's suggestions align with growth goals.
- Documenting changes supports clarity and long-term scalability.
- AI assists with routine scaling but requires careful validation for adaptability.
- Optimistic about AI's role in proactive, efficient scaling.

Riley's Notebook

- Codey's scaling suggestions are helpful but need refinement.
- Maintaining documentation of AI-driven content aids in planning for growth.
- AI can handle routine scaling, letting us focus on complex demands.
- Scaling is smoother with AI as a support, but we still need strategic input.
- Cautiously optimistic about AI's role in scaling our projects.

Bob's Notebook

- AI-driven scaling improves efficiency but requires critical oversight.

- Documentation of AI contributions is key to transparency and clarity.

- Encouraging the team to balance AI with proactive scaling efforts.

- Confident that AI can support long-term growth when used thoughtfully.

- The team's strategic vision remains the foundation of lasting scalability.

Practical Advice

- Use AI tools to assist with routine scaling tasks, such as load balancing and performance monitoring.

- Always validate AI-driven scaling suggestions to ensure alignment with project growth goals.

- Track AI-driven insights and document any modifications for future improvement.

- Balance AI-driven efficiency with adaptability to maintain comprehensive scalability.

- Treat AI as a supportive partner in scaling, using human foresight to guide long-term planning.

Implementation

- Start by using AI for routine scaling tasks, covering basics like load balancing and resource allocation.

- Establish protocols for validating and documenting AI-driven scaling changes.

- Apply AI-driven scaling as a foundation, supplementing it with proactive planning for flexibility and resilience.

- Regularly assess the balance between AI and manual scaling to ensure quality.

- Encourage continuous improvement to refine AI's role in supporting long-term scalability.

Real-World Insight

AI-driven scaling tools, such as Kubernetes and AWS Auto Scaling, help companies manage growth by automating load balancing, resource allocation, and performance monitoring. These tools allow teams to address immediate scaling needs efficiently, freeing up time for strategic planning. However, successful scaling combines AI's efficiency with human foresight, ensuring that growth remains sustainable and adaptable.

Pitfalls to Avoid

- Relying solely on AI for scaling without validating suggestions.

- Failing to document AI-driven scaling changes, leading to missed insights.

- Allowing AI efficiency to overshadow the need for proactive planning.

- Ignoring project-specific requirements in favor of AI-driven scaling.

- Neglecting the need for balanced scaling between AI and human input.

Self-Assessment

- How comfortable am I with using AI for scaling assistance?

- What areas of scaling can AI improve in our workflow?

- How can I ensure AI-driven scaling aligns with project growth goals?

- What strategies can I use to validate AI suggestions effectively?

- How can AI support my role in maintaining high standards in scalability?

Self-Reflection

- Reflect on initial thoughts about AI in scaling—have they evolved?

Chapter 18: AI in Scaling Up – Growth Catalyst or Bottleneck?

- How do you see AI fitting into your scaling workflow going forward?

- Are there aspects of scaling where human oversight is crucial? Why?

- How can AI assist you in becoming more efficient in managing growth?

- What steps can you take to ensure a balanced approach with AI in scaling?

Chapter 19: AI in Innovation – Path to the Future or Risky Gamble?

Chapter 19: AI in Innovation – Path to the Future or Risky Gamble?

Innovation was a key driver of the team's success, pushing them to try new approaches, solve complex problems, and deliver valuable features that set their projects apart. With Codey now well-integrated into their workflow, Bob wanted the team to explore how AI could support them in pushing the boundaries of what was possible, encouraging creativity and experimentation.

"Today, I want us to consider Codey's role in innovation," Bob began. "Let's see if AI can help us generate new ideas, explore different approaches, and maybe even experiment with features we wouldn't have otherwise thought of."

Riley looked intrigued. "So, Codey won't just be supporting our routine tasks? It'll be helping us brainstorm and think creatively?"

"Exactly," Bob replied. "But keep in mind, innovation comes with risks. We need to find a balance between exploring new ideas and keeping our work grounded in the project's goals."

Pat, who was experienced in feature development, agreed. "AI can be a valuable tool for trying out concepts, but we can't lose sight of the project's purpose. Innovation is great, but only if it adds value."

Codey's Role in Supporting Creative Experimentation

To see how Codey could contribute to innovation, Bob asked the team to use AI for brainstorming and prototyping. Codey's initial contributions included:

- **Feature Suggestions**: Codey analyzed recent user feedback and proposed new features that could improve usability, suggesting options like automated shortcuts, enhanced reporting, and interactive tutorials.

- **Alternative Solutions**: For ongoing issues, Codey recommended alternative approaches that the team hadn't previously considered, encouraging them to think outside the box.

- **Prototyping Assistance**: Codey provided basic prototypes for potential features, allowing the team to visualize new ideas and experiment with different designs before committing to development.

Jordan found Codey's feature suggestions inspiring. "These are actually pretty innovative! Some of these ideas might have taken us a while to come up with on our own."

Pat appreciated the alternative solutions Codey suggested for existing issues. "This is helpful. It's easy to get stuck in our usual ways of thinking. Codey's giving us fresh perspectives we might not have considered."

However, Alex expressed caution. "Innovation is great, but Codey's suggestions aren't always realistic or aligned with our project's objectives. We need to ensure we're not pursuing ideas just because they're new and exciting."

Bob agreed, emphasizing the importance of balancing creativity with practicality. "AI can support our creative process, but it's up to us to validate each idea and make sure it's aligned with our goals. Let's use Codey as a springboard, but remember that we're responsible for ensuring every innovation is valuable."

Balancing AI-Driven Innovation with Project Goals

As the team explored Codey's suggestions, they quickly realized that while AI could generate creative ideas, human judgment was essential to filter and refine these concepts. Some of Codey's feature ideas were insightful, but others needed adjustments to fit the project's needs. Additionally, while Codey's alternative solutions were useful, the team found that some required modification to address the project's specific challenges.

Riley found Codey's prototyping assistance particularly helpful, as it allowed the team to visualize ideas and identify potential roadblocks early on. "It's like having a sandbox for new concepts. We can see what works and what doesn't before diving into development."

Pat added, "This is a great way to approach innovation. We can let Codey help us brainstorm, but we need to make sure we're only moving forward with ideas that truly add value."

Bob encouraged the team to use Codey's insights as a foundation for experimentation, applying their expertise to refine and adapt the AI's suggestions. "Innovation is about pushing boundaries, but it's also about delivering value. Let's make sure Codey helps us do both, keeping our ideas grounded in what matters most."

Guidelines for AI-Assisted Innovation

After their session, Bob led the team in establishing best practices for integrating Codey into their innovation process, ensuring that AI-driven creativity enhanced their projects without compromising their goals.

- **Use AI for Brainstorming**: Allow Codey to assist with feature ideas, alternative solutions, and initial prototypes, providing a springboard for experimentation.

- **Validate Each Idea**: Review AI-generated suggestions carefully, ensuring each idea aligns with project goals and adds meaningful value.

- **Document AI Contributions**: Track where AI-driven ideas were implemented and where modifications were made, providing a record of the innovation process.

- **Balance Creativity with Practicality**: Use Codey's insights to inspire new ideas but rely on human expertise to refine and adapt concepts for project needs.

- **Encourage Strategic Experimentation**: Apply AI-driven suggestions as part of a strategic, value-driven approach to innovation, ensuring ideas remain relevant.

"Codey can be a powerful ally in our quest for innovation," Bob concluded, "but true creativity comes from purpose as well as ideas. Let's make sure AI supports our vision without steering us off course."

The team left the meeting with a renewed excitement about how AI could inspire innovation. They knew that while Codey could provide fresh ideas, it was their responsibility to ensure these innovations served the project's goals and delivered meaningful value.

Alex's Notebook

- Codey's innovation suggestions are inspiring, but validation is crucial.

- Documenting AI-driven ideas helps track our innovation process.

- Balancing AI-driven creativity with practicality ensures valuable outcomes.

- AI-driven innovation is exciting, but we need to stay focused on project goals.

- Innovation is about relevance as much as it is about creativity.

Jordan's Notebook

- Codey's feature suggestions inspire fresh ideas for our project.

- Learning from AI's creative approach helps broaden my thinking.

- Documenting AI-driven contributions supports transparency in innovation.

- AI makes innovation feel less intimidating, encouraging experimentation.
- Codey is a helpful partner in our creative efforts.

Pat's Notebook

- AI-driven brainstorming provides useful ideas but needs refinement.
- Maintaining control ensures Codey's suggestions align with project value.
- Documenting changes supports clarity and accountability in innovation.
- AI assists with creative thinking but requires careful validation.
- Optimistic about AI's role in supporting meaningful innovation.

Riley's Notebook

- Codey's creative suggestions are helpful but need adjustment.
- Maintaining documentation of AI-driven content aids in tracking innovation.
- AI can handle brainstorming, letting us focus on refining ideas.
- Innovation is smoother with AI as a support, but we still need oversight.
- Cautiously optimistic about AI's role in fostering valuable ideas.

Bob's Notebook

- AI-driven innovation provides a foundation but requires critical oversight.
- Documentation of AI contributions is key to transparency and alignment.
- Encouraging the team to balance AI with strategic innovation efforts.
- Confident that AI can support creative thinking when used thoughtfully.
- The team's vision remains the foundation of lasting, valuable innovation.

Practical Advice

- Use AI tools to assist with brainstorming and prototyping, supporting creativity.

- Always validate AI-driven innovation suggestions to ensure alignment with project goals.

- Track AI-driven insights and document any modifications for clarity and future reference.

- Balance AI-driven creativity with strategic focus for meaningful innovation.

- Treat AI as a supportive partner in innovation, using human insight to guide creative direction.

Implementation

- Start by using AI for initial brainstorming, feature ideas, and alternative solutions.

- Establish protocols for validating and documenting AI-driven innovation changes.

- Apply AI-driven innovation as a foundation, refining ideas with strategic planning.

- Regularly assess the balance between AI and human input to ensure valuable outcomes.

- Encourage continuous improvement to refine AI's role in supporting creative efforts.

Real-World Insight

AI-driven innovation tools, such as IBM Watson and OpenAI's DALL-E, help companies explore creative solutions by generating feature ideas, alternative approaches, and prototypes. These tools encourage experimentation, broadening the scope of what's possible. However, successful innovation combines AI's creativity with human insight, ensuring that ideas are not only new but also relevant and valuable.

Pitfalls to Avoid

- Relying solely on AI for innovation without validating suggestions.

- Failing to document AI-driven ideas, leading to missed insights.

- Allowing AI creativity to overshadow the need for project alignment.

- Ignoring project-specific requirements in favor of AI-driven ideas.

- Neglecting the need for balanced innovation between AI and human vision.

Self-Assessment

- How comfortable am I with using AI for creative support?

- What areas of innovation can AI improve in our workflow?

- How can I ensure AI-driven ideas align with project goals?

- What strategies can I use to validate AI suggestions effectively?

- How can AI support my role in maintaining high standards in innovation?

Self-Reflection

- Reflect on initial thoughts about AI in innovation—have they evolved?

- How do you see AI fitting into your innovation workflow going forward?

- Are there aspects of innovation where human oversight is crucial? Why?

- How can AI assist you in broadening your thinking and exploring new ideas?

- What steps can you take to ensure a balanced approach with AI in innovation?

Chapter 20: AI in Decision-Making – Empowering or Overstepping?

Chapter 20: AI in Decision-Making – Empowering or Overstepping?

The team had explored how AI could enhance various aspects of their work, from productivity and quality assurance to innovation and scaling. Now, as they neared the end of their journey, Bob wanted to consider a critical question: could Codey assist in decision-making? More importantly, was there a point where AI's role in decision-making could overstep the boundaries of human expertise and intuition?

"To wrap up, I want us to consider how AI influences our decisions," Bob began. "We've seen how Codey can support us, but when it comes to making decisions, how much should we rely on AI?"

Before the team could respond, they were surprised to see Simon enter the room. Smiling, he greeted the group and joined the discussion. "I heard you all were wrapping up your exploration with AI, so I thought I'd drop by and share a few thoughts of my own."

The team welcomed Simon, eager to hear his perspective. They knew that he'd initially been reluctant to embrace AI, and his journey with AI had been cautious and deliberate.

Simon's Evolving Perspective on AI

Simon began by reflecting on his initial skepticism. "When AI was first introduced, I was hesitant. I worried it might dilute our expertise or make us overly dependent. But over time, I've come to see that when AI is used thoughtfully, it can be a powerful ally—especially in making informed decisions."

He shared a recent project where he'd used AI to analyze multiple data points and provide insights that guided his choices. "AI didn't make the decision for me, but it gave me a clearer picture. It supported me without replacing my intuition or judgment."

Alex, who had similar concerns about AI overstepping boundaries, looked intrigued. "So, you're saying AI helps in decision-making, but we have to keep control?"

"Exactly," Simon replied. "AI can empower us with information and insights, but it's up to us to make the final call. Our judgment, experience, and understanding of context—these are things AI can't replicate."

Codey's Role in Decision Support

To see how Codey could support decision-making, Bob set up a scenario for the team, asking Codey to provide data-driven recommendations based on recent performance metrics and user feedback. Codey's contributions included:

- **Data-Driven Insights**: Codey analyzed patterns in user behavior, providing metrics on which features were most popular and where improvements could be made.

- **Risk Assessment**: It highlighted potential risks associated with certain decisions, such as feature removals or changes, offering insights into possible user reactions.

- **Comparative Analysis**: Codey compared various options, highlighting the pros and cons based on data, helping the team weigh their choices.

Jordan found Codey's insights on user behavior helpful. "This data is exactly what we need to make informed decisions. Codey's given us a clear view of the risks and potential rewards."

However, Pat pointed out an important limitation. "While Codey's data is useful, there are nuances it can't account for. Not every decision is about data—some require understanding our team's strengths, user experience, and long-term goals."

Simon agreed, reinforcing the point. "AI can help us make better-informed choices, but it can't replace our intuition. Let's make sure Codey's input enhances our decisions without overshadowing our experience."

Balancing AI-Driven Insights with Human Judgment

As the team reviewed Codey's recommendations, they recognized that while AI-driven insights offered valuable information, decision-making required a holistic approach. Codey's data-driven analysis provided clarity on user behavior and risk assessment, but human judgment was essential for understanding the broader implications.

Riley appreciated Codey's comparative analysis, which helped them weigh their options. "This analysis is useful, especially when we're trying to be objective. But for decisions that affect our team and long-term goals, we need to rely on more than just numbers."

Bob reminded the team of the importance of balance. "AI can empower us with information, but the final decision should always be ours. Codey's insights are tools, not answers. Let's make sure we're using AI to support our decisions without letting it define them."

Guidelines for AI-Assisted Decision-Making

Chapter 20: AI in Decision-Making – Empowering or Overstepping?

After the session, Simon and Bob led the team in establishing best practices for integrating Codey into their decision-making process, ensuring that AI-driven insights enhanced human judgment without overstepping boundaries.

- **Use AI for Data-Driven Insights**: Allow Codey to provide data analysis, risk assessments, and comparisons, supporting a more informed decision-making process.

- **Retain Final Control**: Rely on human expertise to interpret AI-driven insights, using AI as a tool rather than a decision-maker.

- **Document AI Contributions**: Track where AI-driven insights influenced decisions, providing transparency in the decision-making process.

- **Balance Data with Intuition**: Use Codey's insights to support decisions, but prioritize human judgment for complex, context-sensitive choices.

- **Encourage Thoughtful Integration**: Apply AI-driven insights as part of a comprehensive approach to decision-making, ensuring AI complements human understanding.

"Codey can give us data, but our experience is what turns that data into wisdom," Simon concluded. "AI is a powerful tool for decision support, but we're the ones who decide. Let's make sure we're using AI thoughtfully, letting it inform us without losing sight of our own expertise."

The team thanked Simon for his insights, feeling inspired by his journey with AI and encouraged to use Codey responsibly. They left the session with a clear understanding of how to incorporate AI into decision-making without compromising their values or intuition.

Alex's Notebook

- Codey's data-driven insights support decision-making, but human judgment is essential.

- Documenting AI-driven decisions keeps the process transparent.

- Balancing AI analysis with intuition ensures thoughtful decisions.

- AI-driven decision-making is helpful, but we need to stay in control.

- Decision-making is about context, not just data.

Jordan's Notebook

- Codey's insights add depth to our decision-making process.

- Learning from AI's approach broadens my understanding of objective analysis.

- Documenting AI contributions supports accountability in decisions.

- AI makes decision-making feel more grounded, but our intuition is crucial.

- Codey is a supportive tool in our decision-making efforts.

Pat's Notebook

- AI-driven insights offer valuable information but need human oversight.

- Maintaining control ensures Codey's suggestions align with our project goals.

- Documenting changes supports clarity and responsibility in decision-making.

- AI assists with data analysis but requires thoughtful validation.

- Optimistic about AI's role in supporting informed, balanced decisions.

Riley's Notebook

- Codey's decision-making support is helpful but requires refinement.

- Maintaining documentation of AI-driven insights aids in transparent choices.

- AI can handle data-driven analysis, letting us focus on strategic judgment.

- Decision-making is smoother with AI as a support, but we still need oversight.

- Cautiously optimistic about AI's role in empowering wise decisions.

Bob's Notebook

- AI-driven decision-making improves insight but requires critical oversight.

- Documentation of AI contributions is key to transparency and accountability.

- Encouraging the team to balance AI with intuitive decision-making.

- Confident that AI can support choices when used thoughtfully.

- The team's experience and values remain the foundation of sound decisions.

Practical Advice

- Use AI tools to assist with data-driven insights, supporting informed decision-making.

- Always retain control over final decisions to ensure alignment with project goals.

- Track AI-driven insights and document any decision modifications for transparency.

- Balance AI-driven analysis with intuition for comprehensive decision-making.

- Treat AI as a supportive partner in decisions, using human expertise to guide choices.

Implementation

- Start by using AI for initial data analysis and risk assessments to support decisions.

- Establish protocols for validating and documenting AI-driven decision contributions.

- Apply AI-driven insights as a foundation, supplementing with human judgment for complex choices.

- Regularly assess the balance between AI and human input to ensure thoughtful decisions.

- Encourage continuous improvement to refine AI's role in supporting responsible decision-making.

Real-World Insight

AI-driven decision-making tools, such as IBM Watson and Salesforce Einstein, help companies make informed choices by providing data analysis, risk assessments, and trend forecasts. These tools support decision-making efficiency, but successful integration requires balancing AI insights with human expertise, ensuring that decisions are aligned with organizational values and goals.

Pitfalls to Avoid

- Relying solely on AI for decision-making without interpreting insights.

- Failing to document AI-driven decisions, leading to missed transparency.

- Allowing AI analysis to overshadow the need for context-sensitive judgment.

- Ignoring project-specific requirements in favor of AI-driven suggestions.

- Neglecting the need for balanced decision-making between AI and human insight.

Self-Assessment

- How comfortable am I with using AI for decision-making support?

- What areas of decision-making can AI improve in our workflow?

- How can I ensure AI-driven insights align with project goals?

- What strategies can I use to validate AI suggestions effectively?

- How can AI support my role in making thoughtful, informed decisions?

Self-Reflection

- Reflect on initial thoughts about AI in decision-making—have they evolved?

- How do you see AI fitting into your decision-making workflow going forward?

- Are there aspects of decision-making where human oversight is crucial? Why?

- How can AI assist you in making more informed choices?

- What steps can you take to ensure a balanced approach with AI in decision-making?

Chapter 21: Parting Advice

The Team's Journey

From the beginning, the team's journey with Codey has been one of exploration, adaptation, and growth. When Bob first introduced Codey to support their software development workflows, there were mixed reactions. Some, like Jordan, eagerly embraced AI's potential, seeing it as a powerful tool to increase efficiency and innovation. Others, such as Alex, were more cautious, concerned about over-reliance on AI and the impact it could have on team dynamics and decision-making.

Through each chapter, the team encountered unique challenges and opportunities as they integrated Codey into various aspects of their work. They explored how AI could streamline routine tasks, enhance code quality, support creative brainstorming, and provide insights for informed decision-making. Along the way, they learned to balance AI-driven suggestions with human expertise, ensuring that Codey was a partner rather than a replacement.

Simon's final appearance brought a reflective perspective to the team, showing them that AI's role is not to overtake but to empower. The journey wasn't just about implementing an AI tool; it was about evolving their approach to teamwork, creativity, and problem-solving. By the end of their adventure, the team had come to see Codey as a trusted ally, one that supported their goals without compromising their skills, insight, or collaboration.

Encouragement for the Reader

As you reflect on the team's journey with Codey, consider how their experiences can serve as a framework for your own AI-powered adventure. While every organization and team is unique, the lessons shared in this story highlight several important principles:

- **Start with Curiosity, Not Perfection**: Like Bob and his team, allow yourself to experiment and learn as you go. AI is an evolving tool, and your approach will grow with experience.

- **Balance Automation with Expertise**: AI can streamline routine work and improve efficiency, but human expertise is irreplaceable. Use AI to handle tasks that support your goals while allowing your own judgment and skills to guide final decisions.

- **Embrace Collaboration**: AI can enhance teamwork, but clear communication and defined roles remain vital. Keep your team's strengths and goals at the center, and use AI as a tool to reinforce cohesion rather than create distance.

- **Be Strategic About Innovation**: Codey helped the team brainstorm and explore new ideas, but the team made sure each idea added value. When introducing AI, ensure it aligns with your project's purpose and brings meaningful impact.

- **Stay Open to Evolution**: As Simon discovered, initial skepticism can evolve into appreciation. Be open to adjusting your perspective on AI as you see its potential in practice.

Let the team's journey remind you that AI is not an end goal but a means to unlock greater potential in your work. Take these lessons as a foundation, but adapt them to fit your team's unique needs, challenges, and ambitions.

Parting Words of Advice

As you embark on your own AI journey, remember that success with AI doesn't happen overnight. It's a gradual process of learning, testing, and refining, guided by both technical skills and human insight. To help you on this path, keep these key points in mind:

- **Trust Your Instincts**: AI is a powerful tool, but your intuition and experience are what turn data into meaningful action. Trust your instincts as you evaluate AI's suggestions and ensure they align with your goals.

- **Prioritize Clarity and Transparency**: Documenting AI-driven changes, tracking its contributions, and regularly assessing its role in your workflow will ensure that AI enhances rather than disrupts your work. Transparency will also keep your team aligned and informed.

- **Stay Curious and Open to Change**: AI technology continues to evolve, bringing new possibilities and challenges. Stay curious, keep learning, and remain adaptable as you refine your approach to AI-powered development.

- **Remember the Human Element**: AI can handle routine tasks and offer valuable insights, but your team's communication, collaboration, and shared vision are the foundation of every successful project. Use AI to support these qualities, not replace them.

With these principles guiding you, you'll be well-equipped to harness the power of AI in your own software development journey. Let your experiences be a continuous adventure in innovation, driven by both technology and the wisdom that only you and your team bring to the table.

A New Adventure Awaits

As we conclude this AI-powered journey, keep an eye out for the next chapter in the *Adventures in AI-Powered* series. Each new book will explore fresh challenges and opportunities, uncovering how AI can empower teams across different disciplines. With each adventure, we'll dive into the evolving role of AI in the workplace, providing insights, practical tips, and inspiring stories to help you on your path.

So, as you turn the last page of this book, remember that the journey doesn't end here. AI is a powerful tool that, when used thoughtfully, can open doors to new possibilities. Embrace the adventure, apply what you've learned, and continue exploring how AI can transform your work, one project at a time.

Appendix A: Action Plan for Integrating AI into Software Development

Integrating AI into software development is an exciting opportunity, but it requires careful planning and strategic execution. This action plan provides a roadmap to help you thoughtfully incorporate AI into your development processes, maximizing its potential while ensuring it aligns with your goals and values.

Identify Areas for AI Integration

Start by identifying the areas within your software development process where AI can add the most value. Consider where AI could support efficiency, enhance quality, or reduce repetitive tasks, such as:

- Code review and quality assurance

- Testing automation and error detection

- Documentation support

- Data analysis for user feedback and feature prioritization

- Resource management, such as load balancing or scaling

This initial assessment will give you a clear view of where AI can have the most meaningful impact in your workflow.

Set Clear Objectives

Once you've identified potential areas for AI integration, establish clear objectives and success metrics for each. Define what you want AI to achieve in specific terms, such as:

- Reducing the time spent on code reviews by a certain percentage

- Improving testing accuracy and efficiency

- Enhancing documentation consistency

- Accelerating feature development timelines

Setting measurable objectives will help you monitor AI's performance and determine if it's meeting your expectations.

Assess Readiness and Resources

Evaluate your team's current capabilities, resources, and readiness to adopt AI tools. Consider the following factors:

- **Skills and Training**: Does your team need additional training in AI tools or machine learning concepts?

- **Infrastructure**: Does your technology stack support the integration of AI, or are upgrades needed?

- **Budget**: Determine the budget available for AI tools, licenses, and potential infrastructure improvements.

- **Data Availability**: Do you have the data necessary to train or refine AI models effectively?

This assessment will help you identify gaps and prepare your team and technology for AI adoption.

Choose the Right AI Tools

Select AI tools that align with your objectives, team capabilities, and budget. Research and compare AI solutions, considering factors such as:

- **Features**: Does the tool offer the functionalities needed for your specific objectives?

- **Compatibility**: Can it be easily integrated into your current development environment?

- **Ease of Use**: Is the tool user-friendly, and can your team adopt it without a steep learning curve?

- **Support and Updates**: Consider tools with strong customer support and regular updates to ensure longevity.

Selecting the right tools will set the foundation for a smooth integration process and help you avoid unnecessary hurdles.

Pilot and Experiment

Start with a small-scale pilot project to test AI's capabilities and gather initial insights. Focus on one or two areas where AI can have an immediate impact, and use this phase to:

- Observe how AI integrates with your workflows

- Gather feedback from the team on AI's effectiveness and ease of use

- Identify any technical or logistical challenges that may arise

- Assess initial outcomes against your objectives

The pilot phase will provide valuable data and help you refine your approach before a broader rollout.

Monitor and Adapt

As you implement AI more widely, continuously monitor its performance and adapt your approach as needed. Key steps include:

- Regularly reviewing AI-driven outcomes and comparing them to your objectives

- Holding team check-ins to discuss AI's role, effectiveness, and any adjustments needed

- Staying informed on updates and new features for your AI tools

- Adjusting your workflows to improve efficiency and address any emerging challenges

Monitoring and adapting will ensure AI continues to add value without disrupting your team's processes.

Evaluate and Scale

After the initial implementation, evaluate AI's overall impact and determine if it's ready for a larger-scale rollout. Consider:

- **Success Metrics**: Did AI meet or exceed the objectives you set? Document measurable outcomes and specific improvements.

Appendix A: Action Plan for Integrating AI into Software Development

- **Team Feedback**: Gather insights from your team to understand how AI has impacted their roles, productivity, and satisfaction.

- **Scalability**: Assess whether your infrastructure can support AI on a larger scale, and make any necessary adjustments.

If AI has proven successful, develop a plan to scale its integration across additional projects, departments, or processes, keeping your objectives and resources in mind.

Appendix B: Additional Resources for AI-Powered Software Development

For readers looking to further explore AI in software development, this list provides additional resources to support your journey. These materials cover AI fundamentals, hands-on tools, and advanced techniques for integrating AI into software development workflows.

Books

- **Artificial Intelligence: A Guide for Thinking Humans** by Melanie Mitchell
  A comprehensive yet accessible introduction to AI, exploring both technical and ethical dimensions.

- **Machine Learning Yearning** by Andrew Ng
  This free online book offers practical guidance on implementing machine learning projects, authored by one of the field's leading experts.

- **Deep Learning** by Ian Goodfellow, Yoshua Bengio, and Aaron Courville
  A thorough exploration of deep learning, covering both theoretical and practical aspects, ideal for developers who want to understand AI in greater depth.

- **Designing Data-Intensive Applications** by Martin Kleppmann
  While not exclusively about AI, this book provides insights into building scalable, data-driven applications, a critical aspect of integrating AI in development.

- **Hands-On Machine Learning with Scikit-Learn, Keras, and TensorFlow** by Aurélien Géron
  A practical guide focused on using popular libraries to build machine learning models, with hands-on examples and projects.

Online Courses

- **AI For Everyone** by Andrew Ng (Coursera)
  An excellent beginner course, this program introduces the basics of AI and its practical applications across various fields.

- **Deep Learning Specialization** by Andrew Ng (Coursera)
  This series of courses covers deep learning foundations and applications, from neural networks to sequence models.

- **Machine Learning for Software Engineers** by Educative.io
  A course tailored for software engineers, focusing on the practical implementation of machine learning in software development.

- **Data Science and Machine Learning Bootcamp with R** by Jose Portilla (Udemy)
  A beginner-friendly course that uses R to introduce machine learning and data science fundamentals, helpful for those interested in different programming languages for AI.

- **Advanced AI for Developers** by Fast.ai
  This advanced course dives into AI development using deep learning frameworks and provides projects to enhance practical skills.

AI Tools for Developers

- **TensorFlow**
  An open-source platform for machine learning and deep learning, TensorFlow offers a rich ecosystem of libraries and tools for model building and deployment.

- **PyTorch**
  Known for its ease of use and dynamic computation graphs, PyTorch is a favorite among researchers and developers for building neural networks.

- **Keras**
  A high-level API for neural networks, Keras simplifies the process of building and training models, integrating seamlessly with TensorFlow.

- **GitHub Copilot**
  This AI-powered code completion tool assists developers in writing code more efficiently, offering suggestions and completions based on context.

- **Azure Machine Learning**
  A platform from Microsoft for end-to-end machine learning workflows, Azure ML supports data prep, model training, and deployment.

- **Google AI Platform**
  A suite of tools from Google for building, training, and deploying machine learning models at scale, integrated with Google Cloud.

Community Resources

- **Stack Overflow's AI and Machine Learning Communities**
  Connect with other developers to ask questions, share insights, and find solutions to common AI integration challenges.

- **GitHub's Machine Learning Repositories**
  Explore open-source projects and code repositories on GitHub to learn how others are implementing AI in software development.

- **Kaggle**
  Participate in data science competitions, access public datasets, and learn from other practitioners through Kaggle's vibrant community and resources.

- **r/MachineLearning on Reddit**
  A community for sharing news, research, and applications in machine learning, providing a great way to stay updated on AI trends.

- **OpenAI's Research Blog**
  Learn from OpenAI's research insights and project updates to stay informed about AI advancements and new applications.

Industry Publications

- **MIT Technology Review**
  Known for its coverage of cutting-edge technology, MIT Technology Review frequently publishes articles on AI's impact in various industries.

- **AI Magazine**
  Published by the Association for the Advancement of Artificial Intelligence (AAAI), AI Magazine offers in-depth articles on AI research, applications, and developments.

- **The Gradient**
  A publication featuring essays, interviews, and analyses on AI and machine learning, ideal for those looking to delve into technical and philosophical discussions.

- **Journal of Artificial Intelligence Research (JAIR)**
  A scholarly journal for those interested in AI research developments, including advancements in machine learning, NLP, and computer vision.

Appendix B: Additional Resources for AI-Powered Software Development

- **Towards Data Science (Medium Publication)**
  Articles and tutorials contributed by data scientists, developers, and engineers, covering AI, machine learning, and data science topics.

This list of resources serves as a foundation for further exploration, providing tools, insights, and community support to help you continue your AI journey. Whether you're new to AI or looking to deepen your expertise, these materials will equip you with the knowledge and skills needed to integrate AI thoughtfully and effectively into your software development processes.

www.ingramcontent.com/pod-product-compliance
Lightning Source LLC
LaVergne TN
LVHW051338050326
832903LV00031B/3613